A Compassionate Heart

A Compassionate Heart

90 *Our Daily Bread* Reflections
on Sharing the Love of Christ

Bill Crowder

Our Daily Bread
Publishing™

Interior design: Jessica Ess, Hillspring Books

ISBN: 978-1-64070-118-2

Printed in the United States of America

22 23 24 25 26 27 28 / 8 7 6 5 4 3 2

FOREWORD

• • •

What makes a good devotional article? I believe it should lead the reader to the heart of God. It should present the wisdom of Scripture in a way that draws you to better know and love Him.

In my role with putting together *Our Daily Bread,* I've seen Bill Crowder consistently craft articles that point our readers to God— His character, promises, and presence. Bill is a humble servant who possesses a keen theological mind and the heart of a pastor—the heart of a loving shepherd.

As you experience the heart-changing riches found in this book, note how the author has carefully selected illustrations that draw you in and lead you to better understand the Scripture text. Bill carefully combs stories and accounts from history, the news, the arts, and culture to find perfect gems to lead off his articles.

Another thing that marks Bill's devotional writing is his careful use of Scripture. Theological training, years preaching as a pastor and speaking as a Bible teacher, and hour upon hour of personal study have allowed him to know and carefully handle it. But his curious, fertile mind also leads him to humbly search the Scriptures as a true student.

All authors require editing to help polish and perfect their works, and Bill is not immune to receiving suggested edits. He takes the "fixes" seriously and will diligently pore over his devotional articles until they're ready for publication.

Often over the years, Bill has also sent messages or sat down with me to chat about how we can make *Our Daily Bread* articles even better. A consistent discussion point deals with the application. Are we truly pointing readers to God and His wisdom and vast resources or to our own insufficient wisdom and limited resources? I greatly appreciate Bill's tireless pursuit of providing articles that lead you—the reader—to God. Again, he reveals the heart of a loving shepherd.

I've witnessed Bill serving in many different contexts—teaching in camp and conference settings, presenting the Scriptures to the Our Daily Bread Ministries staff, participating in collaborative content meetings, recording programs, and more. He winsomely mixes humor with a drive to do things well and to honor God and the Scriptures. Compassionate and careful. Playful and yet serious. These things come through in both his speaking and his writing as you will find in the following pages.

My wife and I have directed a family camp for many years at a Bible camp in Michigan. We've had the privilege of partnering with Bill and his wife, Marlene, in putting together chapel services for the weeklong camp. Bill's speaking remains a highlight for all who have attended. In fact, my wife will tell you that her all-time favorite Bible teacher is one Bill Crowder. Why? Because, as she says, he makes the Scriptures come alive. And he consistently points you to the heart of *the* Great Shepherd—Jesus.

So what makes a good devotional article? Well, you're about to find out as you are inspired, challenged, and encouraged by *A Compassionate Heart: 90 Our Daily Bread Reflections on Sharing the Love of Christ.* May you be drawn closer to the Shepherd's heart as you read these words from the pen of a loving shepherd.

Tom Felten
Executive Editor
Our Daily Bread

The Privilege

A song I first heard in my earliest days as a follower of Jesus has taken on new meaning for me in recent years. It is the gospel song "Little Is Much When God Is in It." I think I always accepted that as a true statement, but didn't fully comprehend the wonder of it until I started writing for *Our Daily Bread*.

The "little is much" part of the equation is fairly obvious. People have asked me, "How can an article of only 235 words accomplish anything?" It seems foolish, to say the least. Yet, as I began to experience the "when God is in it" part of the song title, I was amazed beyond words. Even more, writing for the *Bread* has been one of the most humbling privileges I have known in my forty-five years of public ministry.

As one of the Bible teachers for Our Daily Bread Ministries (formerly RBC Ministries), I have had the opportunity to travel to countries around the world and speak for Bible conferences. These conferences have been organized and presented by the ODBM teams in those countries, and they are largely focused on ministering to *Our Daily Bread* readers. The result has often been overwhelming.

In Indonesia, a woman stopped me after a service to say that something I had written about the real nature of love had changed her life. Truly, little is much when God is in it, because it couldn't have been my words that could affect that kind of transformation. It is only possible as God empowers His inspired Scriptures to accomplish His desires in a person's heart that we see such results.

One time when I arrived in Nigeria during a season of significant global tensions, I was singled out in the passport control area and subjected to some rather stern questioning by the passport officer. When he asked why I wanted to enter Nigeria, I told him I was there to present a Bible conference for *Our Daily Bread*. Immediately, everything changed! His frown of concern was replaced by a broad smile of brotherhood in Christ, and he shouted, "My family and I read *Our Daily Bread* every evening at the dinner table! Welcome to Nigeria!" Amazing things happen when God is in it.

At a conference in the United States, I encountered a couple whose marriage was radically changed by the simple practice of sharing the *Our Daily Bread* devotional reading and learning to pray together as a couple.

These stories expand exponentially when you read the mail that comes in to the ministry. What I have experienced at global Bible conferences has also been the experience of so many of our writers who hear from senior citizens and children, singles and couples, the happy and the heartbroken, business leaders and prisoners—all saying that somehow God has used the "little" of an *ODB* article to accomplish His good and mighty work in their lives.

It is humbling to have the privilege to be part of such an enterprise, and it is humbling to have these articles of mine gathered together for this special publication. I trust that our faithful Father will use these small offerings to encourage and enrich your heart in the compassion of our Savior. Thanks for reading.

Bill Crowder

· REFLECTIONS ·

A Heart of Concern

Philippians 2:1–11

*In humility, value others above yourselves,
not looking to your own interests but each of you
to the interests of others.* Philippians 2:3–4

Jason Ray was a ray of joy on the University of North Carolina campus in Chapel Hill. He performed as Rameses (the school mascot) for three years, hauling his giant ram's head costume to sporting events one day and children's hospitals the next. Then, in March 2007, while with his team for a basketball tournament, Jason was struck by a car. His family watched and waited at the hospital, but the twenty-one-year-old succumbed to his injuries and died.

His story doesn't end there, however. Jason had filed paperwork two years earlier to donate organs and tissue upon his death—and that act of concern saved the lives of four people and helped dozens of others. A young man in the prime of his life, with everything to live for, was concerned for the well-being of others and acted on that concern. Those individuals who were helped and their families are deeply grateful for this young man who thought of others.

Jason's act echoes the heart of Paul's words in Philippians 2, as he called believers to look beyond themselves and their own interests, and to look to the interests of others. A compassionate heart that turns outward to others will be a healthy heart indeed.

• • •

Looking to the needs of others honors Christ.

Pull Together

Philippians 4:1-3

*Make my joy complete by being like-minded, having
the same love, being one in spirit and of one mind.* Philippians 2:2

A college in our area has an interesting annual rite—a tug-of-war. Two teams train and prepare to pull together on their end of the rope to win the competition, hoping to avoid the mud-pit between the teams and gain campus bragging rights for another year. For a fun competition, it can become intense.

As believers in Jesus, we often face the challenge of learning how to pull together. Self-interest, personal agendas, and power struggles get in the way of genuine ministry and hinder the work of Christ.

Such was the case in Paul's letter to the Philippians, where he had to plead with Euodia and Syntyche to "be of the same mind" (4:2). Their personal friction created a roadblock to their spiritual service, and their "tug-of-war" was harming the life of the church.

Paul's appeal was for them to pull together and work for the honor of the Master. It is an appeal that serves us well today. When we feel distanced from our fellow believers, we must look for the common ground we have in the Savior.

Church is no place for a tug-of-war. It's imperative that we work together for the advancement of God's kingdom. He can use us in wonderful ways when we lay aside our personal differences and pull together on the rope.

• • •

A believer at war with another Christian
cannot be at peace with the Father.

A Time for Compassion

Luke 23:26–34

Jesus said, "Father, forgive them,
for they do not know what they are doing." *Luke 23:34*

In 2002, I was in Jakarta, Indonesia, to teach a two-night Bible conference. The first night, I went to the host church early, and the pastor asked if he could show me around the building. It was impressive in its beauty.

Then the pastor took me to the lower assembly hall. At the front of the hall was a pulpit and a communion table. Behind it was a plain concrete wall on which hung a wooden cross. Below it were some words in the national language of Indonesia. I asked him what the inscription said, and he surprised me by quoting Christ's words from the cross: "Father, forgive them, for they do not know what they are doing" (Luke 23:34).

I asked if it was there for a particular reason, and he said that several years earlier there had been serious rioting in the city, and twenty-one churches were burned to the ground in one day. That wall was all that remained of their former facility—the first of the churches to be torched.

The wall and the verse formed a reminder of the compassion of Christ that He showed on the cross and that became the church's message to their city. Revenge and bitterness will never be a healing response to the hatred and rage of a lost world. But the compassion of Christ definitely is, just as it was 2,000 years ago.

· · ·

Compassion is needed to heal the hurts and hearts of others.

An Expensive Gospel

Philippians 1:19–30

> For it has been granted to you on behalf of Christ
> not only to believe in him, but also to suffer for him. *Philippians 1:29*

On a teaching trip at a Bible institute in another country, my colleague and I were saddened to hear of legislation before the parliament that sought to outlaw the evangelical church. We shared our fears with our students that though we had come to train a generation of pastors, we might instead witness a new wave of persecution. We then joined with the students in prayer and worship to God about the matter.

After we concluded, one of the students said to me, "Thanks for being concerned for us, but don't worry. We've learned that it's not enough for us to preach the gospel or live for the gospel. It is necessary that we suffer for the gospel." His words were not flippant but honest. Living for Christ often exacts a price.

Writing from prison, Paul said, "It has been granted to you on behalf of Christ, not only to believe in him, but also to suffer for him" (Philippians 1:29). His statement is daily lived out by believers around the world who experience hardship and persecution for no greater crime than living openly for the name of Jesus.

Let's pray for God's blessing and protection for our brothers and sisters in Christ who are paying an expensive price for embracing a salvation that is free.

• • •

Those who live for God can expect trouble in the world.

Whom Shall I Send?

Isaiah 6:1–8

I heard the voice of the Lord saying: "Whom shall I send?
And who will go for us?" And I said, "Here am I. Send me!" *Isaiah 6:8*

As a young pastor, I served a fledgling new congregation that included my parents. My father was very active in the church's "people ministries"—evangelism, hospital and nursing-home visitation, bus ministry, relief for the poor, and more. Although he had never been formally trained in ministry, Dad had a natural ability to connect with people who were in the midst of hard times. That was his passion—the downtrodden people who are often overlooked. In fact, on the day he died, my last conversation with him was about someone he had promised to call on. He was concerned that his promise be kept.

I believe that my father's faithful service to others followed the heart of Christ. Jesus looked out over the masses of the forgotten people of the world and felt compassion for them (Matthew 9:36–38). He commanded His followers to pray that the heavenly Father would send workers (like my dad) to reach people weighed down with the cares of life.

My father became the answer to those prayers in many hurting people's lives, and we can be as well. When the prayer goes out for someone to represent Christ's love, may our heart respond: "Lord, here am I. Send me!"

•   •   •

True service is love in working clothes.

Three Friends

*A friend loves at all times, and a brother is born
for a time of adversity.* Proverbs 17:17

The Old Testament characters Job and Daniel had much in common. Both went through serious trials and challenges. Both had great success because of the blessing of God's presence in their lives. Both are viewed as giants of the faith, one for his patience in suffering and the other for his purity in an impure culture.

Job and Daniel had something else in common—each had three significant friends. Here, however, the similarities end. Job's friends became a thorn in his flesh, offering him condemnation when he needed compassion and companionship. As Job struggled with loss and grief, Eliphaz, Bildad, and Zophar seemed bent on intensifying his pain rather than helping him in his adversity.

Daniel's three friends were very different. Taken captive together, Daniel and his companions, Shadrach, Meshach, and Abed-Nego, supported and strengthened one another in difficult times. They stood together in honoring God (Daniel 1), in prayer (2:17–18), and in refusing to bow before the king's image (3:16–18). That's the kind of friend we need.

So what kind of friend am I? Proverbs 17:17 says, "A friend loves at all times." Who needs you to be a friend today?

• • •

A true friend is like support to a leaning wall.

The Heart of Christ

Luke 19:37–44

Oh, that . . . my eyes [were] a fountain of tears!
I would weep day and night for the slain of my people. *Jeremiah 9:1*

I was filling out an online survey when I came to this question: "What is something that is true about you that most people would not guess?" The answer is that I am very sentimental. I get choked up at the movies when the violins start to swell, eyes fill with tears, and the boy finds his long-lost dog—or something comparable. I'm just a softie when it comes to those things.

It's easy and safe to get emotional over fictional characters and events. But it's a different matter to feel deep sadness and grief over real people and their needs. Heartache for the wayward, the suffering, the lost, and the broken tends to mirror the heart and compassion of Jesus, who wept over wayward Jerusalem (Luke 19:41).

When Jeremiah's people were drifting far from God and His love, he also felt the need to weep. He sensed the burden of God's heart and the brokenness of his people. Weeping seemed the only appropriate response (Jeremiah 9:1).

As we see the condition of the fallen world and the lostness of the people who surround us, let's ask God to give us a heart that mirrors the heart of Christ—a heart that weeps with Him for a lost world and then reaches out to them in love.

• • •

True compassion is love in action.

"God Put You in My Way"

Luke 10:30–37

> He wanted to justify himself, so he asked Jesus,
> "And who is my neighbor?" *Luke 10:29*

In the movie *The Four Feathers*, Harry Faversham leaves England in the 1880s to search for his friends in the king's army in the Sudan. In his quest, Harry gets lost and is near death in the vast deserts of Africa. Then, as his life is ebbing away, he is rescued by an African, Abou Fatma, who cares for him.

Stunned by the man's kindness to a stranger, Harry asks why his new friend has done so much for him. Fatma's response is direct: "God put you in my way!"

In the parable of the Good Samaritan, a priest and a religious scholar, whose calling was to help the downtrodden, ignored the need of a fallen traveler who had been left to die on the Jericho Road. A hated Samaritan, however, gave his time and resources to help the hurting man, displaying Christ's compassion. He bandaged his wounds, brought him to an inn, "and took care of him" (Luke 10:34). The ravaged man had been put in the way of all three travelers, but only the Samaritan responded.

As we move through life, we are challenged to respond to the needs of people. We will either show them Christ's love or be indifferent. How will we respond to those God chooses to put in our way?

• • •

Compassion never goes out of fashion.

Silent Witness

Philippians 1:21–27

Conduct yourselves in a manner worthy of the gospel
of Christ. . . . Stand firm in the one Spirit, striving together
as one for the faith of the gospel. *Philippians 1:27*

On a beautiful, warm January morning, a colleague and I were having breakfast in an outdoor coffee shop at MacRitchie Reservoir Park in Singapore. With a beautiful lake and immaculate gardens surrounding us, the setting was quiet, calm, and lovely with a light breeze blowing across the water.

At a nearby table, a young woman sat quietly reading her Bible. She was absorbed in the text, occasionally looking up to consider what she had read. She never said a word, but her heart and priorities were visible to everyone at that coffee shop. It was a gentle, positive, silent witness.

She was not ashamed of Christ or His Book. She neither preached a sermon nor sang a song. She was willing to be identified with the Savior, yet she did not need to announce that allegiance.

In our attempts to share the message of Jesus, we must eventually use words, because ultimately words are needed to present the gospel. But we can also learn from the example of this woman.

There are times when the quietness of our everyday actions speak loudly, revealing our love for the Lord. In our desire to share Christ with a broken world, let's not ignore the power of our silent witness.

•　•　•

Witness for Christ with your life as well as your lips.

Indebted

Romans 1:8–17

*I am obligated both to Greeks and to non-Greeks,
both to the wise and the foolish.* Romans 1:14

The film *Saving Private Ryan*, though disturbingly graphic, tells the gripping story of a World War II rescue squad sent to bring a soldier out of harm's way. One by one the squad members are killed—sacrificed for the life of Private James Ryan. Finally, mortally wounded and near death, the squad leader calls young James close and simply says, "Earn this." Men had given their lives to save Private Ryan, and he needed to embrace the sense of indebtedness such sacrifice should engender. Ryan owed his life to those who had rescued him.

Paul likewise felt indebted. Christ had sacrificed himself to pay for Paul's sins and set him free from judgment and death. Paul's response? "I am obligated both to Greeks and to non-Greeks, both to the wise and the foolish" (Romans 1:14). Why was he indebted to them? The Greeks and barbarians hadn't died for him, nor had the wise or the unwise. But Christ had. The sacrifice of the Son of God on his behalf was so overwhelming to Paul that he felt he owed it to everyone to make sure they heard of God's redeeming love. His sense of indebtedness to Christ made him a debtor to all who needed the Savior.

We can't earn God's gift of love, but we have an obligation to share it with others who need Him.

• • •

We can never sacrifice too much
for Him who sacrificed His all for us.

A Timely Word

Ephesians 4:27–32

A person finds joy in giving an apt reply—
and how good is a timely word! *Proverbs 15:23*

In Liverpool, England, on the eve of the 2006 British Open Championship, professional golfer Graeme McDowell was in trouble. The next day he was going into the tournament clueless about what was causing his struggles on the course.

While he was out for the evening, McDowell got a surprise. A stranger, who was an avid golf fan, recognized him and commented that he had noticed a flaw in his swing. The next day, Graeme tested that advice on the driving range, and to his great shock he discovered that the fan had been correct. Satisfied with the value of the change, Graeme implemented the suggestion and finished the first day of the British Open in first place! All because a stranger took time to speak a word of help.

Words are like that. They are powerful instruments for good or for ill. We can use words in destructive ways, or we can use words to build and encourage. This must be what Solomon had in mind when he said, "A person finds joy in giving an apt reply—and how good is a timely word!" (Proverbs 15:23).

In a world where words are often wielded as weapons, may we use our words as tools to build up the hearts of others.

• • •

Gentle words are more powerful than angry words.

The Hospitality Manager

Romans 12:9–21

Share with the Lord's people who are in need.
Practice hospitality. *Romans 12:13*

Victoria's family refers to her as the "hospitality manager" of their home. She lives in Singapore with her daughter and son-in-law. He is the Our Daily Bread Ministries international director, and they often have visitors. Victoria stays busy as a volunteer in the ODB Ministries office on that island nation, but her primary ministry is the gift of caring and hospitality. She makes their visitors feel welcome, loved, and cared for in their home.

The word *hospitality* means "love of strangers," and this is precisely what the apostle Paul was calling us to in Romans 12. In the midst of the practical challenges to believers about our relationship with God and one another, Paul said that we are to "share with the Lord's people who are in need. Practice hospitality" (v. 13). This may call us outside our comfort zone to show love and care to those the Lord brings across our path. Hebrews 13:2 adds this intriguing thought about hospitality: "Do not forget to show hospitality to strangers, for by so doing some people have shown hospitality to angels without knowing it."

Often overlooked and sometimes unappreciated, the ministry of the "hospitality manager" is a great gift, and it brings with it the added possibility of surprising blessings along the way!

• • •

To stretch your soul, reach out with Jesus's love.

A New Purpose

Mark 1:16–22

"Come, follow me," Jesus said, "and I will send
you out to fish for people." *Mark 1:17*

Jacob Davis was a tailor with a problem. It was the height of the Gold Rush in the American West of the 1800s and the gold miners' work pants kept wearing out. Davis's solution? He went to a local dry goods company owned by Levi Strauss, purchased tent cloth, and made work pants from that heavy, sturdy material—and blue jeans were born. Today, denim jeans in a variety of forms (including Levi's) are among the most popular clothing items in the world, and it's all because tent material was given a new purpose.

Simon and his friends were fishermen on the Sea of Galilee. Then Jesus arrived and called them to follow Him. He gave them a new purpose. No longer would they fish for fish. As Jesus told them, "Come, follow me, . . . and I will send you out to fish for people" (Mark 1:17).

With this new purpose set for their lives, these men were taught and trained by Jesus so that, after His ascension, they could be used by God to capture the hearts of people with the message of the cross and resurrection of Christ. Today, we follow in their steps as we share the good news of Christ's love and salvation.

May our lives both declare and exhibit this love that can change the lives, purposes, and eternal destinies of others.

• • •

With our new life in Christ we have been given a new purpose.

An Eternal Perspective

*Set your mind on things above,
not on earthly things.* Colossians 3:2

In the movie *Gladiator*, General Maximus Decimus Meridius seeks to stir his cavalry to fight well in the imminent battle against Germania. Addressing his troops, he challenges them to give their very best. He makes this profound statement: "What we do in life echoes in eternity."

These words from a fictional military leader convey a powerful concept that is of particular significance to believers in Christ. We are not just taking up time and space on a rock that's floating in the universe. We are here with the opportunity to make an eternal difference with our lives.

Jesus himself said, "Store up for yourselves treasures in heaven, where moths and vermin do not destroy, and where thieves do not break in and steal" (Matthew 6:20). Having the perspective of living for eternity can make all the difference in this world.

How can we learn to set our minds "on things above" (Colossians 3:2)? A good way to begin is to discover what our eternal God values. Throughout the pages of the Bible, He reminds us that He values people above possessions and our character above our performance. Those are the truths that last forever. Embracing them can bring an eternal perspective to our daily living.

• • •

What we do in this life echoes in eternity.

The Kindness
of Strangers

Philippians 2:1–8

Do not forget to show hospitality to strangers,
for by so doing some people have shown hospitality
to angels without knowing it. Hebrews 13:2

While I was taking a flight to Surabaya, Indonesia, for a Bible conference, the flight attendants brought meal service. I had just eaten in the Singapore airport, so I declined, asking only for a soft drink. The Indonesian man next to me, a stranger, was visibly concerned.

The man asked if I felt okay, and I assured him I was fine. He then asked if perhaps the meal didn't appeal to me. I responded that I just wasn't hungry. He then surprised me by offering his own meal to me, thinking that if I tried it I might actually enjoy it. It was done in such a gentle and genuine way that it was obviously an expression of his concern for my welfare.

In a self-centered world where we are conditioned to look out for our own interests above and beyond all else, such kindness was unexpected. The man's simple gesture showed a different kind of heart and a different set of values. As followers of Christ, we are called to model a similar counter-cultural attitude toward life (Philippians 2:1–8).

In Hebrews 13:2 we read, "Do not forget to show hospitality to strangers, for by so doing some people have shown hospitality to angels without knowing it." What better way to represent Christ than with kindness—even to strangers.

• • •

Kindness is one gift anyone can give.

A Question of Motive

Hebrews 4:11–16

*The word of God is alive and active. Sharper than
any double-edged sword . . . it judges the thoughts
and attitudes of the heart.* Hebrews 4:12

My wife and I were stopped at a railroad crossing to allow a train to pass. As we waited in the line of cars, the driver next to us suddenly darted through a nearby parking lot and headed in the direction of the next available railroad crossing.

I turned to Marlene and said, with some righteous indignation, "Look at that guy. He's trying to get around the train instead of waiting like the rest of us." As soon as I said those words, the man, camera in hand, hopped from his car to take pictures of the oncoming train. I had judged his motives, and I was dead wrong.

Although we can observe behavior and outward appearance, only God can see what's in the heart. That is one reason we all need the Word of God so desperately. Hebrews 4:12 says, "For the word of God is alive and active. Sharper than any double-edged sword, it penetrates even to dividing the soul and spirit, joints and marrow; it judges the thoughts and attitudes of the heart."

When we find ourselves ready to judge another person's motives, let's pause and remember—only God can see the heart, and only His Word can expose its motives. Our responsibility is to let the Lord and His Word convict us about our own hearts.

• • •

People will be judged by the way God sees them—
not by the way we see them.

Little Things

James 3:1–12

The tongue is a small part of the body,
but it makes great boasts. *James 3:5*

A mosquito is a tiny insect—but its potential for devastation is huge. When I was in the fifth grade, I was bitten by mosquitoes on both of my knees. The bites became infected and deteriorated into a threatening case of blood poisoning. For over a month, I was pricked repeatedly with penicillin shots, and my knees had to be lanced and drained twice daily to remove the infection. It was excruciatingly painful, and quite terrifying for a ten-year-old kid. To this day, I carry scars on my knees from the numerous lancings. All because of something as tiny as a mosquito.

James, the half-brother of Jesus, warns us of another little thing that can be destructive. He says that even though the tongue is little, it boasts great things. It's like a small spark that sets a great forest on fire (3:5). Although the tongue is small, there is nothing small about the damage it can do. Words carry with them the power of healing or a destructive capacity far greater than the poison of any mosquito bite.

It is essential that we use our words with great wisdom and care. Consider carefully the words you choose. Will they be seasoned with the balm of grace or with the poison of anger?

• • •

It is better to bite your tongue than to let it bite someone else.

A Church That Cares

Philippians 2:1–11

Let each of you look out not only for his own interests, but also for the interests of others. Philippians 2:4 (NKJV)

While traveling together, my wife and I started talking with a delightful young woman we met. The time passed quickly as we chatted about lighthearted topics. But when she heard that I was a minister, the conversation took a heart-wrenching turn. She began to share with us that when her husband left her only a few months earlier, she had struggled with the pain of that abandonment.

Then she smiled and said, "I can't tell you how much my church has meant to me these past months." Her mood and countenance changed dramatically as she recounted the ways her church family had wrapped their loving arms around her in her season of heartache. It was refreshing to hear how that local assembly had surrounded her with the love of Christ.

Far too often it seems we limit the significance of church to what happens on Sunday, but the church is to be so much more. It is to be a safe haven, a rescue station, and a training center for spiritual service. The church is to be many things, but it is particularly to be an expression of the concerned heart of the Lord for hurting, broken people, such as our young friend. We are called to "love one another" (1 John 4:7).

· · ·

Hope can be ignited by a spark of encouragement.

The Richness of Humility

1 Corinthians 3:1–10

Neither the one who plants nor the one who waters is anything, but only God, who makes things grow. 1 Corinthians 3:7

She lived out spiritual humility, yet she had much on a human level to be proud of. As an author of over seventy books and a translator of many others into Afrikaans, Annalou Marais had much cause to brag—but she was more concerned about honoring Christ than advancing herself. I saw her working behind the scenes of a Bible conference, doing a servant's tasks with a smile. It would have been natural for her to desire, and even deserve, the spotlight. Instead, she quietly served, joyfully weeping as God worked in people's hearts. It was an impressive humility, because it was completely genuine.

I have heard it said, "It is amazing what can be accomplished when we don't care who gets the credit." This is certainly true of Christian service. Paul told the church at Corinth, "I planted the seed, Apollos watered it, but God has been making it grow. So neither the one who plants nor the one who waters is anything, but only God, who makes things grow" (1 Corinthians 3:6–7). Paul had learned that great lesson of the servant's heart, as Annalou has learned—it's entirely about God. What we do is accomplished by His power and grace, and all the glory must go to Him.

It was a lesson in humility watching Annalou—one that reminded me of the richness of serving God.

• • •

Pride and grace cannot dwell in the same place.

Flawed and Frail

1 Corinthians 1:18–31

God chose the foolish things of the world
to shame the wise. *1 Corinthians 1:27*

One of my boyhood heroes was American frontiersman Davy Crockett, the "King of the Wild Frontier." I looked up to him, admiring his courage and exploits.

Years later, my brother gave me a book that traced the experiences of the real-life David Crockett. I was surprised by his humanness. The real Davy Crockett made mistakes and had serious personal problems. The book depicted him as both flawed and frail.

This was disappointing but reassuring to me. It was disappointing because he was less than I had come to believe but reassuring because that reality made Crockett more accessible to me—and even more of a hero.

In the Bible we see that God consistently used people who were far less than perfect. That shouldn't surprise us. God is glorified by showing himself strong through our weaknesses. It shows us that He desires to work through our lives not because we are perfect but because He is. And since He uses weak and foolish things (1 Corinthians 1:27), it means you and I are prime candidates for His work.

The Lord isn't looking for superheroes. He uses those of us who are flawed and frail, so He can show His strength and grace. He wants people with a willing and available heart.

. . .

In God's service, our greatest ability is our availability.

Choosing the Hard Thing

2 Corinthians 4:5–18

We are hard pressed on every side, but not crushed;
perplexed, but not in despair. 2 Corinthians 4:8

On September 12, 1962, President John F. Kennedy delivered a speech at Rice University in Houston, Texas, about the difficult challenges facing the nation. He also shared his passion for the United States to place a man on the moon.

In balancing the needs of his people with the desire to conquer space, Kennedy said, "We choose to go to the moon in this decade. We choose to go to the moon and do the other things, not because they are easy but because they are hard." The nation responded. Seven years later, Neil Armstrong took a "giant leap for mankind" in July of 1969, walking on the moon.

Today's world is filled with energy-saving devices that make life easier, but there is something to be said for embracing life's challenges. The apostle Paul found serving Christ hard, but he didn't see it as a cause for discouragement. He continued to focus on Christ, and wrote, "We are hard pressed on every side, but not crushed; perplexed, but not in despair" (2 Corinthians 4:8). Paul knew that "the one who raised the Lord Jesus from the dead will also raise us with Jesus and present us with you to himself" (v. 14). The goal was worth the pain.

By the grace of God, may we commit to serving Jesus—not just when it's easy, but when it's hard.

• • •

Jesus gave His all to save us.
Are we giving our all to serve Him?

Passionate Boldness

Acts 4:5–13

> When they saw the courage of Peter and John, . . .
> they were astonished and they took note
> that these men had been with Jesus. *Acts 4:13*

A young man was preaching to the passersby in Hounslow, on the outskirts of London, England. Most ignored him, a few ridiculed, and several stopped to listen. But regardless of the reaction of the people, he was undeterred. With a strong voice and clear resolve, he poured out his heart—not with the words of an angry prophet, but with deep concern for the men and women on that street. His eyes, facial expressions, and tone of voice revealed an attitude of compassion, not condemnation. In it all, he boldly shared the love and grace of Jesus Christ.

In Acts 4, when the church was still new, Peter and John also boldly addressed the people of their generation. The response of the leaders of their day? "Now when they saw the courage of Peter and John and realized that they were unschooled, ordinary men, they were astonished and they took note that these men had been with Jesus" (v. 13). That boldness was not the fruit of ministerial training but of much time spent in the presence of the Master. As a result, they had become passionate about what concerned Christ—the eternal destiny of men and women.

That same passionate boldness was on the face of the young man in Hounslow. Do people see it in us?

· · ·

A Christian is an ambassador who speaks for the King of kings.

The Best Mum

Proverbs 31

Her children arise and call her blessed;
her husband also, and he praises her. *Proverbs 31:28*

A few years ago, British national television ran an intriguing story. Peggy Bush's daughter had died, so Peggy absorbed the responsibility of caring for her daughter's three children while her son-in-law worked. Then, tragically, her son-in-law also died. With both parents gone, Peggy took her three grandchildren in and raised them.

In a world where wrong is glamorized and the lurid is presented as appealing, we seldom hear of the good things that happen. Yet this woman's love and sacrifice were recognized, acknowledged, and honored as the nation took note of her as Britain's "Best Mum" for that year.

Most of the efforts, sacrifices, and expressions of love our mothers have given us will not be the lead story on the news. Their recognition will be more personal. But what matters is not the scope of the appreciation but its genuineness.

How important it is that we thank God for the mothers who have molded our hearts. As we honor them, we fulfill the truth of Proverbs 31:28, "Her children arise and call her blessed; her husband also, and he praises her."

• • •

Nothing touches a child like a mother's love.

Be a Stander

2 Timothy 4:9–18

A friend loves at all times, and a brother is born
for a time of adversity. *Proverbs 17:17*

Western novelist Stephen Bly said that in the days of America's Old West there were two types of friends (and horses): runners and standers. At the first sign of trouble, the runner would bolt—abandoning you to whatever peril you were facing. But a stander would stick with you no matter the circumstances. Unfortunately, you wouldn't know which kind of friend you had until trouble came. And then it was too late—unless your friend was a stander.

Rather than being concerned with what kind of friends we *have*, however, we ought to consider what kind of friends we *are*. In the final days of Paul's ministry, as he awaited death, some who had ministered with him turned into runners and abandoned him to face execution alone. In his last letter, he listed some (like Demas) who had run off, then simply stated, "Only Luke is with me" (2 Timothy 4:11). Luke was a stander. While undoubtedly disappointed by those who had deserted him, Paul must have been deeply comforted to know he was not alone.

Proverbs tells us that "a friend loves at all times" (17:17). During times of adversity, we need friends we can rely on. When the people we know face trouble, what kind of friend will we be—a runner or a stander?

•   •   •

A true friend stands with us in times of trial.

The Review

2 Corinthians 5:1–11

We must all appear before the judgment seat of Christ,
so that each of us may receive what is due us for the things
done while in the body, whether good or bad. *2 Corinthians 5:10*

Imagine going to work one day and being greeted by your boss, who says, "Come by my office at 9:30. I'd like to talk to you about how you're doing on the job."

This could be a nervous time for you as you think about what your supervisor might say. You wonder, How does my boss think I've been doing? Could there be a promotion with a pay increase? Could I lose my job? Am I going to hear, "Well done" or "You're done"?

As important as this kind of meeting is, the Bible speaks of another, far more significant review. After this life is past, we will stand before our Lord. Paul wrote, "We must all appear before the judgment seat of Christ, so that each of us may receive what is due us for the things done while in the body, whether good or bad" (2 Corinthians 5:10). We will not enter that future evaluation fearful of losing our salvation, nor will we desire personal benefit or human approval. Instead, we will be eager to hear the Master say, "Well done, good and faithful servant!" (Matthew 25:21).

The challenge before us as followers of Christ is to serve Him with excellence now so we can hear His words, "Well done" then. Based on the way I am living today, what kind of review will I get when I see the Savior?

• • •

Service done well here on earth
will receive a "Well done" in heaven.

I, Me, Mine

Philippians 2:1–11

Do nothing out of selfish ambition or vain conceit. Philippians 2:3

In 1970, the Beatles began work on a documentary intended to show how their music was made. But instead of revealing the process of musical creativity, the film pulled the curtain back on a display of self-interest and bickering. The band members were more concerned about their own songs than the advancement of the group. Shortly after the project was completed, the group dissolved in disharmony and broken friendships.

It's an age-old problem. In the first century AD, the apostle Paul feared that the believers in the church at Philippi would fall into the trap of selfishness. He knew that when the desire for personal advancement overrides concern for one another, attitudes quickly become disruptive and divisive.

To counteract this dangerous tendency, Paul wrote, "Do nothing out of selfish ambition or vain conceit. Rather, in humility value others above yourselves, not looking to your own interests but each of you to the interests of others" (Philippians 2:3–4).

What would a documentary of your life reveal? Selfishness or selflessness? We must look out for one another, for selfless concern will prevent division and build unity in our church families.

• • •

A heart that is focused on others will not be consumed with self.

Life's Surprises

1 Samuel 16:1–7

> The LORD does not look at the things people look at.
> People look at the outward appearance,
> but the LORD looks at the heart. *1 Samuel 16:7*

No one watching *Britain's Got Talent* (a popular televised talent show) expected much when mobile phone salesman Paul Potts took the stage. The judges looked skeptically at one another when the nervous, unassuming, ordinary-looking chap announced he would sing opera—until Potts opened his mouth.

He began to sing Puccini's "Nessun Dorma"—and it was magical! The crowd roared and stood in amazement while the judges sat stunned in tearful silence. It was one of the greatest surprises any such television program has ever had, in large part because it came wrapped in such an ordinary package.

In the Old Testament, the rescuer of Israel arrived at the battlefield in a most unlikely form—a young shepherd boy (1 Samuel 17). King Saul and his entire army were surprised when David defeated Goliath and won the day. They needed to learn the way that God looks at people. He said to the prophet Samuel, "The LORD does not look at things people look at. People look at the outward appearance, but the LORD looks at the heart" (16:7).

If we judge others only by their outer appearance, we might miss the wonderful surprise of what's in their heart.

• • •

It's what's in the heart that counts.

What's It All About?

Romans 9:1–5

*I could wish that I myself were cursed and cut off from Christ
for the sake of my people, those of my own race.* Romans 9:3

Recently I was in a crowded shopping area when I saw a woman plowing her way through the crowd. What intrigued me was the message on her T-shirt, which read in bold capital letters, IT'S ALL ABOUT ME. Her actions reinforced the words on her shirt.

I'm afraid she's not alone. That message is declared by so many men and women today that it could be the motto of our modern world. For followers of Christ, however, that statement simply is not true. It is not all about us—it's all about Jesus Christ and others.

The apostle Paul certainly felt the weight of this reality. He was so concerned that his fellow Israelites would know Christ that he said, "I could wish that I myself were cursed and cut off from Christ for the sake of my people, those of my own race" (Romans 9:3). That is a remarkable statement! Far from thinking it was all about himself, Paul affirmed that he would willingly exchange his eternity for theirs.

Paul's teaching is a refreshing reminder of self-sacrifice in a challenging world that is destructively self-centered. The question we must ask is this: Is it all about me? Or is our life about Jesus Christ and the people He came to reach?

Think about it. What's it all about?

• • •

Our lives should be marked by love for Christ and others—
not obsession with self.

A Lasting Imprint

Matthew 5:13–30

Let your light shine before others,
that they may see your good deeds
and glorify your Father in heaven. *Matthew 5:16*

Caerleon is a Welsh village with deep historical roots. It was one of three sites in the United Kingdom where Roman legions were posted during Rome's occupation of Britain. While the military presence ended some 1,500 years ago, the imprint of that occupation can still be seen today. People come from all over the world to visit the military fort, the barracks, and the amphitheater that are reminders of the days when Rome ruled the world and occupied Wales.

It amazes me that fifteen centuries later, the evidence of Rome's presence can still so clearly be seen in that small community.

I wonder, though, about another kind of imprint—the imprint of Christ on our lives. Do we allow His presence to be clearly seen by others? Is it possible for people who interact with us to know that Jesus occupies our lives?

Jesus calls us to make known His presence in our lives to the glory of God the Father. He says, "Let your light shine before others, that they may see your good deeds and glorify your Father in heaven" (Matthew 5:16). Through the light of our testimony and the impact of our deeds of service, people should be able to see evidence of the presence of God in our lives. Is it true? Can they see His imprint?

. . .

Let your testimony be written in large enough letters
so the world can always read it.

Tone Check

Colossians 4:2–6

*Let your conversation be always full of grace, seasoned with salt,
so that you may know how to answer everyone.* Colossians 4:6

Driving home from work, I heard a radio advertisement that got my attention. It was for a computer program that checks emails as they are written. I was familiar with "spell check" and "grammar check" programs, but this was different. This was "tone check." The software monitors the tone and wording of emails to make certain they are not overly aggressive, unkind, or mean-spirited.

As I listened to the announcer describe the features of this software, I wondered what it would be like to have something like that for my mouth. How many times have I reacted harshly instead of listening first—and later regretted the words I had spoken? Certainly, a tone check would have protected me from responding so foolishly.

Paul saw the need for us as believers to check our speech—especially when talking to those who are not Christians. He said, "Let your conversation be always full of grace, seasoned with salt, so that you may know how to answer everyone" (Colossians 4:6). His concern was that our speech be graceful, reflecting the beauty of our Savior. And it must be inviting to others. Talking with the right tone to unbelievers is vital to our ability to witness to them. Colossians 4:6 can be our tone check.

• • •

Every time we speak, our heart is on parade.

A Debt of Gratitude

Romans 16:1–16

They risked their lives for me. Not only I but all the churches
of the Gentiles are grateful to them. *Romans 16:4*

Dave Randlett was someone of whom I can say, "Because of him, my life will never be the same." Dave, who went to heaven in October 2010, became a mentor to me when I was a new follower of Jesus in my college years. He not only invested time in me but he also took risks by giving me opportunities to learn and grow in ministry. Dave was God's instrument to give me the opportunity to be a student preacher and travel with a college music team. As a result, he helped shape and prepare me for a life of teaching God's Word. I'm glad I was able to express thanks to him on a number of occasions.

Just as I am thankful for Dave's influence in my life, the apostle Paul was grateful for Aquila and Priscilla, who served the Lord with him. He said they "risked their lives for me." In gratitude, he thanked them, as did "all the churches of the Gentiles" (Romans 16:4).

You too may have people in your life who have taken risks by giving you opportunities to serve or who have greatly influenced you spiritually. Perhaps pastors, ministry leaders, friends, or family members have given of themselves to move you further along for Christ. The question is, have you thanked them?

• • •

For those who have helped you, take time to give them thanks.

Becoming Bilingual

Acts 17:19–31

"In him we live and move and have our being." As some of your own poets have said, "We are his offspring." *Acts 17:28*

Is it possible—in a society that seems increasingly indifferent to the gospel—to communicate the good news to people who don't share our faith?

One way to connect with people who are unfamiliar with the things of Christ is to become culturally "bilingual." We do this by communicating in ways people can easily relate to. Knowing about and discussing music, film, sports, and television, for example, can offer just such an opportunity. If people hear us "speak their language," without endorsing or condoning the media or events we refer to, it could open the door to sharing the timeless message of Christ.

Paul gave us an example of this in Acts 17. While visiting the Areopagus in Athens, he spoke to a thoroughly secular culture by quoting pagan Greek poets as a point of reference for the spiritual values he sought to communicate. He said, "'In him we live and move and have our being.' As some of your own poets have said, 'We are his offspring'" (Acts 17:28). Just as Paul addressed that culture by knowing what they were reading, we may have greater impact for the gospel by relating it to people in terms they can readily embrace.

Are you trying to reach a neighbor or a coworker with the gospel? Try becoming bilingual.

．　．　．

The content of the Bible must be brought
into contact with the world.

Feeding Frenzy

Matthew 5:1–12

Blessed are the merciful,
for they will be shown mercy. *Matthew 5:7*

People who study sharks tell us that they are most likely to attack when they sense blood in the water. The blood acts as a trigger to their feeding mechanism, and they attack, often in a group, creating a deadly feeding frenzy. Blood in the water marks the vulnerability of the target.

Sadly, this is sometimes how people in the church respond to those who are hurting. Instead of being a community where people are loved, cared for, and nurtured, it can become a dangerous environment where predators are looking for the "blood in the water" of someone's failings or faults. And then the feeding frenzy is on.

Instead of kicking people when they are down, we should be offering the encouragement of Christ by helping to restore the fallen. Of course, we're not to condone sinful behavior, but our Lord calls us to display mercy. He said, "Blessed are the merciful, for they will be shown mercy" (Matthew 5:7). Mercy has been described as not getting what we deserve, and we all deserve eternal judgment. The same God who shows us mercy in Christ calls us to show mercy to one another.

When we see "blood in the water," let's seek to show mercy. The day may come when we will want someone to show mercy to us!

• • •

We can stop showing mercy to others
when Christ stops showing mercy to us.

The Greatest

Matthew 22:34–40

*"Love the Lord your God with all your heart
and with all your soul and with all your mind."
This is the first and greatest commandment.* Matthew 22:37–38

What is the greatest thing in sports? Is it championships? Records? Honors? In the Palestra, the University of Pennsylvania basketball arena, a plaque offers a different perspective on the greatest thing in sports. It reads: "To win the game is great. To play the game is greater. But to love the game is the greatest of all." This is a refreshing reminder that sports are, after all, just the games we played with joy as kids.

A religious leader once asked Jesus about greatness: "Which is the greatest commandment?" (Matthew 22:36). Jesus responded by challenging that leader to love—love God and love others. Jesus said, "'Love the Lord your God with all your heart and with all your soul and with all your mind.' This is the first and greatest commandment. And the second is like it: 'Love your neighbor as yourself'" (Matthew 22:37–39).

Whatever else our faith in Christ compels us to do, there is nothing greater we can do than to show our love—for love reveals the heart of our holy heavenly Father. After all, "God is love" (1 John 4:8). It's easy to be sidetracked by lesser things, but our focus must remain on the greatest thing—loving our God. That in turn enables us to love one another. There's nothing greater.

. . .

The proof of our love for God
is our obedience to the commands of God.

True Religion

James 1:19–27

> Religion that God our Father accepts as pure and faultless is this:
> to look after orphans and widows in their distress and to keep
> oneself from being polluted by the world. *James 1:27*

I recently saw an ad for a brand of clothing geared toward youth. It consists of blue jeans and all the accessories designed to go with them. There is nothing novel about that. What got my attention, however, was the name of this clothing line. It is called "True Religion." That caused me to stop and think. Why was that name chosen? Am I missing some deeper significance? What is the connection between a brand of jeans and true religion? What do they mean by it? My musings left me with questions for which I had no answers.

I am thankful that the book of James is clear when describing true religion or true faith: "Religion that God our Father accepts as pure and faultless is this: to look after orphans and widows in their distress and to keep oneself from being polluted by the world" (1:27). That is refreshing. "True religion"—genuine faith—is an expression of how we relate to our God. One evidence of our new identity in Christ is the way we care for one another—reaching to the most frail and vulnerable among us, to those most in need of help.

True religion is not a garment to be taken on and off. It is a lofty challenge about how we live before a holy God and others.

· · ·

You don't advertise your religion by wearing a label—
you do it by living a life.

A Sense of Concern

Galatians 2:1–10

*Whoever oppresses the poor shows contempt for their Maker,
but whoever is kind to the needy honors God.* Proverbs 14:31

Statistics are tricky. While numbers give us information, sometimes they can also desensitize us to the people those numbers represent. This hit me recently as I read a statistic: Every year fifteen million people die from hunger. That's chilling, and for those of us who live in cultures of plenty, it's hard to fathom. In one recent year, nearly nine million children died before their fifth birthday, with a third of those deaths related to hunger. These are staggering numbers, but they are much more than numbers. They are individuals loved by God.

We can show the Father's heart of love by responding to people's physical needs. Solomon wrote, "Whoever oppresses the poor shows contempt for their Maker, but whoever is kind to the needy honors God" (Proverbs 14:31). We can show mercy to the needy by volunteering at a soup kitchen, assisting in a job search, financially supporting the drilling of wells in places that need fresh water, distributing food in poverty-stricken regions, teaching a trade, or providing lunches for school children.

Accepting this responsibility honors the Father and His concern for all. And those who are starving might be better able to hear the message of the cross if their stomachs aren't growling.

• • •

**The more we understand God's love for us
the more love we'll show to others.**

Careless Speech

James 3:1–12

*The one who has knowledge uses words with restraint,
and whoever has understanding is even-tempered.* Proverbs 17:27

When my wife and I were visiting a church for a special musical program, we arrived early to get a good seat. Before the program began, we overheard two members seated behind us complaining about their church. They criticized the pastoral staff, leadership, music, ministry priorities, and several other things that made them unhappy. They were either unconcerned about or oblivious to the presence of two visitors in their midst.

It occurred to me that their unfortunate conversation could have pushed us away if we were there looking for a new church home. Worse, what if we were seeking God, and their disgruntled opinions had driven us away? Their careless speech was not just a matter of the words they used or attitudes they displayed, but it also demonstrated their lack of concern for the impact those words could have on others.

A better approach to the use of words is reflected in Proverbs 17:27, where Solomon said, "The one who has knowledge uses words with restraint, and whoever has understanding is even-tempered." Most often, we would do better not to say all we think or know (or think we know), but instead seek to use words that promote calm and peace. You never know who may be listening.

. . .

Discretion of speech is better than eloquence with words.

A Growing Belligerence

Philippians 4:4–9

If it is possible, as far as it depends on you,
live at peace with everyone. *Romans 12:18*

On a recent trip, the flight attendant asked if I flew very often. When I said I did, he asked, "Have you noticed people on planes becoming increasingly more belligerent and aggressive in recent months?" I had to confess that I agreed with him. We began talking about what might be contributing to it—things like increased airport security, higher costs, fewer services, and a general dissatisfaction with travel. As if to prove the point, our conversation was interrupted by a passenger who refused to sit in his assigned seat because he liked someone else's seat assignment better!

When we encounter anger and belligerence, the follower of Christ can be a peacemaker. Paul wrote to the church at Rome with this challenge, "If it is possible, as far as it depends on you, live at peace with everyone" (Romans 12:18). What does that mean? For one thing, it means that we must control what we can control. We can't control the attitudes of others, but we can control our response.

When we see angry or hostile attitudes displayed around us, we can show the heart of the Prince of Peace by responding graciously in a peaceful manner. In this way we will demonstrate the attitude of our Savior in a world filled with a growing belligerence.

• • •

The world needs a peace that passes all misunderstanding.

They Are Watching

Matthew 5:13–16

*Let your light shine before others, that they may see your
good deeds and glorify your Father in heaven.* Matthew 5:16

A professional football player's team was having a terrible season, losing week after week. A reporter asked him how he stayed motivated to play hard and give his best even though his team lost almost every game. He responded, "My dad is watching that game. My mom is watching that game. You better believe I'm going to do my best!" He recognized that there was more at stake than just winning or losing. People were watching, and that reality always drove him to do his best.

Jesus reminded us of this reality in the early portions of His Sermon on the Mount. We should live our lives with a recognition that what we do is observed by those around us—and this visible life makes a statement about our God. He said, "Let your light shine before others, that they may see your good deeds and glorify your Father in heaven" (Matthew 5:16). How does the light of our lives shine? By bringing the heart and character of Christ into the situations that engage us every day. By showing compassion as He did for the marginalized or forgotten. By displaying concern for the Father's name and reputation.

People are watching us. The question is, "What do they see?"

• • •

Let your light shine—whether you're a candle
in a corner or a lighthouse on a hill.

To the End

Acts 1:1–8

You will be my witnesses in Jerusalem, and in all Judea
and Samaria, and to the ends of the earth. *Acts 1:8*

It was my first day of class at the Moscow Bible Institute where I
was teaching Russian pastors. I began by asking the students to give
their names and where they served, but one student shocked me as
he boldly declared, "Of all the pastors, I am the most faithful to the
Great Commission!" I was taken aback momentarily until, smiling,
he continued, "The Great Commission says we are to take the gospel
to the ends of the earth. I pastor north of the Arctic Circle in a village nicknamed 'The End of the Earth'!" Everyone laughed and we
continued with the session.

The words of that pastor, who ministered in the Yamal (which
means "end of the world") Peninsula, carry great significance. In
Jesus's final message to His disciples, He said, "You will be my witnesses in Jerusalem, and in all Judea and Samaria, and to the ends
of the earth" (Acts 1:8). Every corner of our world, no matter how
remote, must be touched by the message of the cross. The Savior died
for the world—and that includes people both near and far.

Each of us has the opportunity to take the gospel to people in our
"[end] of the earth." No matter where you are, you can tell someone
about the love of Christ. Who can you tell today?

• • •

Any place can be the right place to witness for Christ.

Making a Difference

Matthew 9:27–38

When [Jesus] saw the crowds,
he had compassion on them. *Matthew 9:36*

Elizabeth's story was moving, to say the least. Following a terribly humiliating experience in Massachusetts, she caught a bus to New Jersey to escape her embarrassment. Weeping uncontrollably, she hardly noticed that the bus had made a stop along the way. A passenger sitting behind her, a total stranger, began making his way off the bus when he suddenly stopped, turned, and walked back to Elizabeth. He saw her tears and handed her his Bible, saying that he thought she might need it. He was right. But not only did she need the Bible, she needed the Christ it speaks of. Elizabeth received Him as a result of this simple act of compassion by a stranger who gave a gift.

Jesus is our example of compassion. In Matthew 9, we read, "When he saw the crowds, he had compassion on them, because they were harassed and helpless, like sheep without a shepherd" (v. 36). Not only did our Lord notice the pain and hurt of broken people but He also responded to it by challenging His followers to pray for the Father to send out workers to respond to the hurts and needs of this dying world (v. 38).

As we follow Christ's example, a heart of compassion for shepherdless people can compel us to make a difference in the lives of others.

• • •

A world in despair needs Christians who care.

True Hospitality

Revelation 22:16–21

Let the one who is thirsty come; and let the one who wishes take the free gift of the water of life. Revelation 22:17

In 1987, our family moved to California to take up the pastorate of a church in the Long Beach area. The day we flew into town, my secretary picked us up at the airport to take us to our house. As we pulled into traffic, the very first thing I saw was a bumper sticker that read: "Welcome to California . . . Now Go Home!" It was not exactly a warm and cheery welcome to sunny Southern California!

I wonder if there might be occasions in our lives when we send similar signals to people around us. Whether we are at church, in the neighborhood, or at social gatherings, are there times when we fail to make others feel welcome in our world?

In Romans 12:13, Paul instructed his readers to "practice hospitality." The book of Hebrews goes even further, saying, "Do not forget to show hospitality to strangers, for by so doing some people have shown hospitality to angels without knowing it" (13:2). By showing gracious kindness to those who come our way, we echo the Savior's invitation for salvation, which declares, "Let the one who is thirsty come; and let the one who wishes take the free gift of the water of life." (Revelation 22:17).

To show someone loving hospitality just might be the first step in showing that person the way to heaven.

• • •

**Live so that when people get to know you,
they will want to get to know Christ.**

What We Talk About

Psalm 19

May these words of my mouth and this meditation
of my heart be pleasing in your sight, LORD. *Psalm 19:14*

Perhaps you are familiar with the saying, "Great minds discuss ideas; average minds discuss events; small minds discuss people." Admittedly, there are ways to speak of people that can honor them. But this saying highlights our darker experiences. In a world of ever-present media—social and professional—we are continually confronted with people's lives at a level of intimacy that can be inappropriate.

Worse, this tidal wave of personal information about others could become grist for our conversational mills to the point that gossip becomes the norm—and not just about the rich and famous. People in our workplaces, churches, neighborhoods, and families can also be targets of sharp tongues and feel the pain of discussions that never should have happened.

How can we escape our inclination to use words to hurt others? By recognizing that the ultimate Hearer of our words is God, who longs for us to be better than that. With the psalmist, we can pray, "May these words of my mouth and this meditation of my heart be pleasing in your sight, LORD" (Psalm 19:14). When we seek to please God with our conversations about others, we honor Him. With His help, we can glorify Him through what we talk about.

• • •

It is better to bite your tongue than to make a biting remark.

The Wisdom of Crowds

1 Corinthians 1:18–25

For lack of guidance a nation falls,
but victory is won through many advisers. *Proverbs 11:14*

The online description of *The Wisdom of Crowds* reads, "In this fascinating book, *New Yorker* business columnist James Surowiecki explores a deceptively simple idea: Large groups of people are smarter than an elite few, no matter how brilliant—better at solving problems, fostering innovation, coming to wise decisions, even predicting the future."

The author uses a variety of things, ranging from pop culture to politics, to present one basic thought: More often than not, the crowd gets it right. It's an interesting theory, but one that would probably be debated during election years or when someone's favorite contestant is voted off a reality TV show.

While the Bible makes it clear that the wisdom of crowds may not be reliable and can be dangerous (Matthew 7:13–14), there is another way collective wisdom can be helpful. In Proverbs 11:14, we read, "For lack of guidance a nation falls, but victory is won through many advisers." One of the benefits of the body of Christ is that we can assist one another—in part by working together to seek God's wisdom. When we join together to pursue God's purposes, we find safety in His provision of each other and receive His wisdom for the challenges of life.

• • •

We best pursue the wisdom of God when we pursue it together.

Overwhelming Concern

John 13:31–35

A new command I give you:
Love one another. *John 13:34*

A while ago, I wrote an article about my wife, Marlene, and her struggles with vertigo. When the article appeared, I was unprepared for the tidal wave of response from readers offering encouragement, help, suggestions and, mostly, concern for her well-being. These messages came from all over the world and from people in all walks of life. Expressions of loving concern for my wife poured in to the point where we could not even begin to answer them all. It was overwhelming in the best kind of way to see the body of Christ respond to Marlene's struggle. We were, and remain, deeply grateful.

At its core, this is how the body of Christ is supposed to work. Loving concern for our brothers and sisters in the Lord becomes the evidence that we have experienced His love. While addressing the disciples at the Last Supper, Jesus said, "A new command I give you: Love one another. As I have loved you, so you must love one another. By this everyone will know that you are my disciples" (John 13:34–35).

Marlene and I experienced a sampling of Christlike love and concern in those letters we received. With the help of our Savior and as a way of praising Him, may we show others that kind of love as well.

• • •

The height of our love for God is indicated by the depth
of our love for one another. —Patrick Morley

Being a Witness

Acts 1:1–9

You will receive power when the Holy Spirit comes on you;
and you will be my witnesses. *Acts 1:8*

When I was a teen, I witnessed an auto accident. It was a shocking experience that was compounded by what followed. As the only witness to the incident, I spent the ensuing months telling a series of lawyers and insurance adjustors what I had seen. I was not expected to explain the physics of the wreck or the details of the medical trauma. I was asked to tell only what I had witnessed.

As followers of Christ, we are called to be witnesses of what Jesus has done in us and for us. To point people to Christ, we don't need to be able to explain every theological issue or answer every question. What we must do is explain what we have witnessed in our own lives through the cross and the resurrection of the Savior. Even better is that we don't have to rely on ourselves alone to do this. Jesus said, "You will receive power when the Holy Spirit comes on you; and you will be my witnesses in Jerusalem, and in all Judea and Samaria, and to the ends of the earth" (Acts 1:8).

As we rely on the Spirit's power, we can point the way for a hurting world to find the redeeming Christ. With His help, we can be a witness to the life-changing power of His presence in our lives!

• • •

Our testimony is the witness of what God has done for us.

Genuine Concern

Philippians 2:1–5

*Let each of you look out not only for his own interests,
but also for the interests of others. Philippians 2:4 (NKJV)*

On the first night at family camp, the camp director informed the families of the schedule for the week. When finished, he asked if anyone else had anything to say. A young girl stood up and made a passionate appeal for help. She shared about her little brother—a boy with special needs—and how he could be a challenge to care for. She talked about how tiring this was for her family, and she asked everyone there to help them keep an eye on him during the week. It was an appeal born out of genuine concern for her brother and her parents. As the week went on, it was great to see people pitching in to help this family.

Her appeal was a gentle reminder of how easily we can all get wrapped up in our own world, life, and problems—to the point that we fail to see the needs of others. Here's how Paul described our responsibility: "Let each of you look out not only for his own interests, but also for the interests of others" (Philippians 2:4 NKJV). The next verse reminds us that this is part of the example of Christ: "Let this mind be in you which was also in Christ Jesus" (NKJV).

Caring for others displays a Christlike concern for people who are hurting. May we rest in God's grace, trusting Him to enable us to serve others in their seasons of need.

• • •

Nothing costs as much as caring—except not caring.

Gentle Witness

Acts 1:1–11

You will be my witnesses in Jerusalem,
and in all Judea and Samaria, and to the ends of the earth. *Acts 1:8*

Years ago, I was hospitalized following a life-threatening, thirty-eight-foot fall from a bridge. While I was in the hospital, the wife of the man in the next bed stopped to speak to me. "My husband just told me what happened to you," she said. "We believe God spared your life because He wants to use you. We've been praying for you."

I was stunned. I had grown up going to church, but I had never imagined that God would want to be involved in my life. Her words pointed me to a Savior I had heard of but did not know—and marked the beginning of my coming to Christ. I cherish the memory of those words from a gentle witness who cared enough to say something to a stranger about the God whose love is real. Her words conveyed care and concern, and offered purpose and promise.

Jesus challenged His disciples—and us—to tell others about the love of God: "You will receive power when the Holy Spirit comes on you; and you will be my witnesses in Jerusalem, and in all Judea and Samaria, and to the ends of the earth" (Acts 1:8).

Through the Holy Spirit our words and witness can have the power to make an eternal difference in the lives of others.

• • •

A caring word can accomplish more than we could ever imagine.

Probing Questions

1 Peter 3:8–17

Always be prepared to give an answer to everyone who asks you to give the reason for the hope that you have. 1 Peter 3:15

While riding on a train a few years after the American Civil War, General Lew Wallace of the Union Army encountered a fellow officer, Colonel Robert Ingersoll. Ingersoll was one of the nineteenth-century's leading agnostics, and Wallace was a man of faith. As their conversation turned to their spiritual differences, Wallace realized that he wasn't able to answer the questions and doubts raised by Ingersoll. Embarrassed by his lack of understanding about his own faith, Wallace began searching the Scriptures for answers. The result was his confident declaration of the person of the Savior in his classic historical novel *Ben-Hur: A Tale of the Christ.*

Probing questions from skeptics don't have to be a threat to our faith. Instead, they can motivate us to seek a deeper understanding and equip us to respond wisely and lovingly to those who might question our faith. The apostle Peter encouraged us to pursue the wisdom of God in the Scriptures when he wrote, "Always be prepared to give an answer to everyone who asks you to give the reason for the hope that you have" (1 Peter 3:15).

We don't have to have an answer for every question, but we need the courage, confidence, and conviction to share our love for Christ and the hope that is in us.

• • •

Christ is the ultimate answer to life's greatest questions.

Family Trademarks

1 John 4:7–16

Dear friends, let us love one another, for love comes from God.
Everyone who loves has been born of God and knows God. *1 John 4:7*

The Aran Islands, off the west coast of Ireland, are known for their beautiful sweaters. Patterns are woven into the fabric using sheep's wool to craft the garments. Many of them relate to the culture and folklore of these small islands, but some are more personal. Each family on the islands has its own trademark pattern, which is so distinctive it is said that if a fisherman were to drown he could be identified simply by examining his sweater for the family trademark.

In John's first letter, the apostle describes things that are to be trademarks of those who are members of God's family. In 1 John 3:1, John affirms that we are indeed part of God's family by saying, "See what great love the Father has lavished on us, that we should be called children of God!" He then describes the trademarks of those who are the children of God, including, "Dear friends, let us love one another, for love comes from God. Everyone who loves has been born of God and knows God" (4:7).

Because "love comes from God," the chief way to reflect the heart of the Father is by displaying the love that characterizes Him. May we allow His love to reach out to others through us—for love is one of our family trademarks.

. . .

Love is the family resemblance the world
should see in followers of Christ.

City of Refuge

Psalm 59:10–17

I will sing of your strength, in the morning I will sing of your love;
for you are my fortress, my refuge in times of trouble. *Psalm 59:16*

As we entered a town in Australia, we were greeted by a sign that declared: "We welcome all who are seeking refuge and asylum." This kind of welcome seems to resonate with the Old Testament concept of the cities of refuge. In the Old Testament era, cities of refuge (Numbers 35:6) were established to be a safe haven for people who had accidentally killed someone and needed protection. God had the people establish such cities to provide that refuge.

This concept, however, was not intended to be simply a practice for ancient Israel. More than that, cities of refuge reflected the heart of God for all people. He himself longs to be our safe haven and our city of refuge in the failures, heartaches, and losses of life. We read in Psalm 59:16–17, "I will sing of your strength, in the morning I will sing of your love; for you are my fortress, my refuge in times of trouble. You are my strength, I sing praise to you; you, God, are my fortress, my God on whom I can rely."

For the hurting heart of every generation, our "city of refuge" is not a place. Our city of refuge is a Person—the God who loves us with an everlasting love. May we find our refuge and rest in Him.

• • •

Refuge can be found in the Rock of Ages.

Human Chess

1 John 4:7–12

Dear friends, let us love one another, for love comes from God.
Everyone who loves has been born of God and knows God. *1 John 4:7*

Chess is an ancient game of strategy. Each player begins with sixteen pieces on the chessboard with the goal of cornering his opponent's king. It has taken different forms over the years. One form is human chess, which was introduced around AD 735 by Charles Martel, a ruler in Austrasia. Martel would play the game on giant boards with real people as the pieces. The human pieces were costumed to reflect their status on the board and moved at the whim of the players—manipulating them to their own ends.

Could this human version of the game of chess be one that we sometimes play? We can easily become so driven by our goals that people become just one more pawn we use to achieve them. The Scriptures, however, call us to a different view of those around us. We are to see people as created in the image of God (Genesis 1:26). They are objects of God's love (John 3:16) and deserving of ours as well.

The apostle John wrote, "Dear friends, let us love one another, for love comes from God. Everyone who loves has been born of God and knows God" (1 John 4:7). Because God first loved us, we are to respond by loving Him and the people He created in His image.

• • •

People are to be loved, not used.

Building a Bridge

1 Thessalonians 1:1–10

Your faith in God has become known everywhere.
Therefore we do not need to say anything about it. 1 Thessalonians 1:8

James Michener's *Centennial* is a fictional account of the history and settlement of the American West. Through the eyes of a French-Canadian trader named Pasquinel, Michener converges the stories of the Arapaho of the Great Plains and the European-based community of St. Louis. As this rugged adventurer moves between the growing clutter of the city and the wide-open spaces of the plains, he becomes a bridge between two drastically different worlds.

Followers of Christ also have the opportunity to build bridges between two very different worlds—those who know and follow Jesus and those who do not know Him. Early Christians in Thessalonica had been building bridges to their idol-worshiping culture, so Paul said of them, "The Lord's message rang out from you not only in Macedonia and Achaia—your faith in God has become known everywhere" (1 Thessalonians 1:8). The bridge they were building had two components: the "Lord's message" and the example of their faith. It was clear to everyone that they had "turned to God from idols to serve the living and true God" (v. 9).

As God declares himself to those around us by His Word and through our lives, we can become a bridge to those who do not yet know the love of Christ.

• • •

Live the gospel and others will listen.

The Unlikely

1 Corinthians 1:25–31

God chose the foolish things of the world
to shame the wise; God chose the weak things of the world
to shame the strong. *1 Corinthians 1:27*

Frances Kemble was a British actress who moved to America in the early 1800s and married a southern plantation owner named Pierce Butler. Frances enjoyed the life afforded by the wealth of the plantation, until she saw the cost of that luxury—a cost paid by the slaves who worked her husband's plantations.

Having written a memoir of the cruel treatment slaves often suffered, Kemble was eventually divorced from her husband. Her writings were widely circulated among abolitionists and published in 1863 as *Journal of a Residence on a Georgian Plantation in 1838–1839*. Because of her opposition to slavery, the former wife of a slave owner became known as "The Unlikely Abolitionist."

In the body of Christ, God often wonderfully surprises us. He regularly uses the unlikely—people and circumstances—to accomplish His purposes. Paul wrote, "But God chose the foolish things of the world to shame the wise; God chose the weak things of the world to shame the strong. God chose the lowly things of this world and the despised things—and the things that are not—to nullify the things that are" (1 Corinthians 1:27–28).

This reminds us that God, in His grace, can use anyone. If we will allow His work to be done in us, we might be surprised at what He can do through us!

• • •

God desires willing hearts ready to be used.

The Waving Girl

Romans 15:1–7

Accept one another, then, just as Christ accepted you,
in order to bring praise to God. Romans 15:7

In the late 1800s and early 1900s, a familiar sight greeted ships as they pulled into the port of Savannah, Georgia. That sight was Florence Martus, "The Waving Girl." For forty-four years, Florence greeted the great ships from around the world, waving a handkerchief by day or a lantern by night. Today, a statue of Florence and her faithful dog stands in Savannah's Morrell Park, permanently welcoming incoming vessels.

There is something in a warm welcome that speaks of acceptance. In Romans 15:7, Paul urged his readers: "Accept one another, then, just as Christ accepted you." Paul had in view our treatment of each other as followers of Christ, for in verses five and six he challenged us to live in harmony with one another. The key is to have "the same attitude of mind toward each other that Christ Jesus had, so that with one mind and one voice you may glorify the God and Father of our Lord Jesus Christ" (vv. 5–6).

Our acceptance of our fellow believers in Christ demonstrates more than just our love for each other—it reflects the great love of the One who has permanently welcomed us into His family.

• • •

The closer Christians get to Christ,
the closer they get to one another.

Opening Doors

Matthew 28:16–20

Therefore go and make disciples of all nations. Matthew 28:19

Charlie Sifford is an important name in American sports. He became the first African American playing member of the Professional Golfers Association (PGA) Tour, joining a sport that, until 1961, had a "whites only" clause in its bylaws. Enduring racial injustice and harassment, Sifford earned his place at the game's highest level, won two tournaments, and in 2004 was the first African American inducted into the World Golf Hall of Fame. Charlie Sifford opened the doors of professional golf for players of all ethnicities.

Opening doors is also a theme at the heart of the gospel mission. Jesus said, "Therefore go and make disciples of all nations, baptizing them in the name of the Father and of the Son and of the Holy Spirit, and teaching them to obey everything I have commanded you. And surely I am with you always, to the very end of the age" (Matthew 28:19–20).

The word *nations* (v. 19) is from the Greek word *ethnos*, which is also the source of the word *ethnic*. In other words, "Go and make disciples of all ethnicities." Jesus's work on the cross opened the way to the Father for everyone.

Now we have the privilege of caring for others as God has cared for us. We can open the door for someone who never dreamed they'd be welcomed personally into the house and family of God.

• • •

Jesus opened the doors of salvation to all who will believe.

A Treasure to Be Shared

2 Corinthians 4:1–7

We have this treasure in jars of clay to show that this
all-surpassing power is from God and not from us. *2 Corinthians 4:7*

In March 1974, Chinese farmers were digging a well when they made a surprising discovery: Buried under the dry ground of central China was the Terracotta Army—life-size terracotta sculptures that dated back to the third century BC. In this extraordinary find were some 8,000 soldiers, 150 cavalry horses, and 130 chariots drawn by 520 horses. The Terracotta Army has become one of the most popular tourist sites in China, attracting over a million visitors annually. This amazing treasure lay hidden for centuries but is now being shared with the world.

The apostle Paul wrote that followers of Christ have a treasure inside them that is to be shared with the world: "We now have this light shining in our hearts, but we ourselves are like fragile clay jars containing this great treasure" (2 Corinthians 4:7 NLT). The treasure inside us is the message of Christ and His love.

This treasure is not to be hidden but is to be shared so that by God's love and grace people of every nation can be welcomed into His family. May we, through His Spirit's working, share that treasure with someone today.

• • •

Let others see your testimony as well as hear it.

Campaign of Reconciliation

Luke 19:1–10

"The Son of Man came to seek and to save the lost." *Luke 19:10*

In Craig Nelson's book *The First Heroes*, we read about the Doolittle Raiders, who launched the first major counterattack on the Pacific front during World War II. Not all of the "raiders" returned from their bombing mission. Jacob DeShazer was among those who were captured and held in Japanese POW camps under difficult and painful circumstances.

DeShazer later went back to Japan after the war, but not to seek revenge. He had received Jesus as his Savior and had come back to Japanese soil carrying the message of Christ. A former warrior who was once on a campaign of war had returned on a campaign of reconciliation.

DeShazer's mission to Japan mirrors the heart of the Savior, who himself came on a mission of love and reconciliation. Luke reminds us that when Christ came into the world, it was not merely to be a moral example or a compelling teacher. He came "to seek and to save the lost" (19:10). His love for us found its expression in the cross, and His rescue of us found its realization when He emerged triumphantly from the tomb in resurrected life.

In Christ we find forgiveness, and that forgiveness changes our life and our eternity—all because Jesus came on a campaign of reconciliation.

• • •

We can go to others because Jesus came to us.

Actions Speak Louder

Matthew 9:1–8

Dear children, let us not love with words or speech
but with actions and in truth. *1 John 3:18*

Irritated with a young athlete who had accomplished little yet boasted about his ability, a TV commentator said, "Don't tell me what you're going to do—tell me what you've done!" Actions speak louder than words.

This principle is seen in Jesus's life. In Matthew 9, a paralytic was brought to Him. Jesus's response? "Your sins are forgiven" (v. 2). When the religious leaders objected, He raised the question of the hour: "Which is easier: to say, 'Your sins are forgiven,' or to say, 'Get up and walk'?" (v. 5).

The answer is obvious. To say He had forgiven the man's sins was simple, because it couldn't be proven or disproven. But to say "Get up and walk" was different. It was instantly verifiable. So to prove His authority to forgive sins, Jesus said to the paralytic, "Get up, take your mat and go home" (v. 6). And he did!

Jesus's actions supported His words, and so should ours. John wrote, "Dear children, let us not love with words or speech but with actions and in truth" (1 John 3:18). What we say is significant to a watching world only if it's consistent with what we do. As we tell people about Christ's love, those words will communicate powerfully if surrounded by acts of love and kindness. Actions do speak louder!

• • •

Our works and words should say the same thing.

Doing Well

James 2:1–13

*If you really keep the royal law found in Scripture,
"Love your neighbor as yourself," you are doing right.* James 2:8

In the book *Flags of Our Fathers*, James Bradley recounts the World War II battle of Iwo Jima and its famous flag-raising on Mount Suribachi. Bradley's father, John, was one of the flag-raisers. But more important, he was a Navy corpsman—a medic.

In the heat of battle, facing a barrage of bullets from both sides, Bradley exposed himself to danger so he could care for the wounded and dying. This self-sacrifice showed his willingness and determination to care for others, even though it meant placing himself at great personal risk.

Doc Bradley was awarded the Navy Cross for his heroism and valor, but he never spoke of it to his family. In fact, it was only after his death that they learned of his military decorations. To Doc, it wasn't about earning medals; it was about caring for his buddies.

In James 2:8 we read: "If you really keep the royal law found in Scripture, 'Love your neighbor as yourself,' you are doing right." By intentionally seeking to care for others in the way we would hope to be treated, James says we "are doing right."

Selflessly "doing right" expresses the heart of God, and it fulfills His law of love.

• • •

Love is at the heart of obedience.

The Ushpizin

Matthew 5:21–26

*Religion that God our Father accepts as pure and faultless is this:
to look after orphans and widows in their distress and to keep
oneself from being polluted by the world.* James 1:27

In Jewish legend, the ushpizin are guests who visit the pious at Sukkot, the Feast of Tabernacles. They are supposedly the great Old Testament heroes who come offering comfort and encouragement to the faithful.

According to Jewish lore, these unseen guests only visit the sukkah (shelter) where the poor are welcome—a reminder of each person's responsibility to care for others. It also reminds them that unseen watchers may be observing their conduct.

The story of the ushpizin isn't true, of course. But beyond the lore and legend we are reminded that we as Christ-followers are living observed lives. Others are watching us. And our concern for others, particularly the least among us, is an expression of the compassion Christ displayed to the hurting and outcast of His generation.

James, the half-brother of Jesus, challenged believers to put the love of Christ into practice. He wrote, "Religion that God our Father accepts as pure and faultless is this: to look after orphans and widows in their distress and to keep oneself from being polluted by the world" (James 1:27).

The example of Christ and the words of Scripture inspire us to care for our hurting world. Who's watching us? Our world is watching. And so is our Lord!

· · ·

When people observe your life, do they see the love of Christ?

So Others May Live

Romans 9:1–5

I could wish that I myself were cursed and cut off from Christ
for the sake of my people, those of my own race. *Romans 9:3*

In the movie *The Guardian*, the viewer is taken into the world of United States Coast Guard rescue swimmers. Eighteen weeks of intense training prepares these courageous men and women for the task of jumping from helicopters to rescue people in danger at sea. The challenges they face include hypothermia and death by drowning. Why would people risk so much for strangers? The answer is found in the rescue swimmer's motto, "So Others May Live."

In *Foxe's Book of Martyrs*, we read of a different kind of rescue that demanded extreme commitment and sacrifice. John Foxe recorded the stories of believers who suffered and died because they proclaimed the love of Jesus. Knowing it could cost them their lives, these believers made the Savior known to a world in desperate need of Him.

The apostle Paul, himself a martyr for Christ, expressed his passion for the hearts of people this way, "I could wish that I myself were cursed and cut off from Christ for the sake of my people, those of my own race" (Romans 9:3). Paul so longed for his fellow Jews to come to Christ that he was willing to sacrifice all, "so others may live."

May we likewise embrace this passion for the eternal souls of men and women.

• • •

The cross reveals God's heart for the lost.

The Brevity of Life

Psalm 90

Our days may come to seventy years, . . .
yet the best of them are but trouble and sorrow,
for they quickly pass, and we fly away. *Psalm 90:10*

On October 19, 2008, I heard the news that Levi Stubbs, lead singer for Motown's vocal group The Four Tops, had died at age seventy-two. As a boy, I enjoyed the Four Tops, especially Stubbs's emotion-filled, passionate voice. I had never met him or heard the group in concert, yet his passing affected me at an unexpected level.

Behind my sadness, I think, was the reminder that I too am getting older. The death of someone I listened to when I was young reminded me that time isn't marching on—it's running out!

In the only psalm attributed to Moses, he wrote, "Our days may come to seventy years, . . . yet the best of them are but trouble and sorrow, for they quickly pass, and we fly away" (90:10). Those aren't words we want to hear. We want to remain forever young, but Scripture reminds us that the years pass and death will one day arrive.

That leaves us to wrestle with two essential questions: Am I ready to "fly away" at life's end, having trusted Christ as my Savior? And am I using my fleeting days to please the One who loves me eternally?

How are you doing—no matter what your age—with the challenges raised by the brevity of life?

. . .

You can't control the length of your life,
but you can control its depth.

The Right People

1 Corinthians 12:7–18

God has placed the parts in the body, every one of them,
just as he wanted them to be. *1 Corinthians 12:18*

The film *Miracle* tells the true story of the 1980 US Olympic ice hockey team as it marches to an improbable gold medal. At the outset of the story, coach Herb Brooks is shown selecting the players for his team. When he gives assistant coach Craig Patrick a list of names he has chosen, Craig says in surprise, "You're missing some of the best players." Brooks responds, "I'm not looking for the best players, Craig—just the right ones."

Brooks knew that individual talent would take the team only so far. A willingness to fit into his style of selfless play would be far more important than talent. Clearly, team success, not individual glory, was the priority.

The biblical call to service has a similar emphasis. In God's purposes, each believer does his or her part, but the results are team-oriented. After explaining the wide differences in the spiritual gifts of believers, Paul says, "to each one the manifestation of the Spirit is given for the common good" (1 Corinthians 12:7). When we use the skills God gives us, His purposes are accomplished, and He gets the glory. In God's service, it's not about being the best, the most talented, or the most gifted. It's about being the right people—the ones God "placed . . . in the body" (v. 18)—joining together to serve the same team.

• • •

There are no unimportant people in the body of Christ.

Retreating Forward

Matthew 14:13–23

After he had dismissed them, he went up
on a mountainside by himself to pray.
Later that night, he was there alone. *Matthew 14:23*

A friend told me about his church's leadership retreat. For two days, church leaders pulled away for a time of prayer, planning, and worship. My friend was not only refreshed but also energized. He told me, "This retreat is really going to help us move forward as a church ministry."

It sounded funny to me—this notion of retreating in order to move forward. But it is true. Sometimes you have to pull back and regroup before you can make meaningful forward progress. This is particularly true in our relationship with God.

Jesus himself practiced "retreating forward." After a busy day of ministry in the region of the Sea of Galilee, He retreated. Matthew 14:23 tells us that after He dismissed the crowd, "he went up on a mountainside by himself to pray. Later that night, he was there alone." Alone in the presence of the Father.

In this fast-paced, get-ahead world, it's easy to wear ourselves down—pressing ahead and moving forward at all costs. But even in our desire to be effective Christians, we must consistently be willing to retreat into God's presence. Only in the refreshing of His strength can we find the resources to move forward in our service for Him. Retreat in Jesus before moving forward.

· · ·

Alone with the Father is the only place
to find the strength to press on.

The Forgotten Worker

Hebrews 6:9–20

> God is not unjust; he will not forget your work
> and the love you have shown him as you have helped
> his people and continue to help them. *Hebrews 6:10*

People around the world are familiar with Mount Rushmore, the South Dakota site where the heads of four US presidents are carved in gigantic scale on a cliff wall. Yet, while millions know of Mount Rushmore, relatively few know the name Doane Robinson—the South Dakota state historian who conceived the idea of the magnificent sculpture and managed the project. The monument is admired and appreciated, but he is the forgotten man behind the masterpiece. His name is either largely unrecognized or was never even known by some.

Sometimes, in the service of the Master, we may feel that we have been forgotten or are behind the scenes and not recognized. Ministry can be a life of effort that often goes unappreciated by the very people we are seeking to serve in Jesus's name. The good news, however, is that, while people may not know, God does. Hebrews 6:10 says, "God is not unjust; he will not forget your work and the love you have shown him as you have helped his people and continue to help them."

What a promise! Our heavenly Father will never forget our service to Him. That is infinitely more important than being applauded by the crowds.

· · ·

Serving to please Christ is a greater reward than public acclaim.

First Impressions

John 7:14–24

Stop judging by mere appearances,
but instead judge correctly. *John 7:24*

A while back, *Our Daily Bread* published an article I wrote about a young woman who wore a T-shirt that said, "Love Is for Losers." In it, I commented on what a sad message that was, and I wrote about the hurt this motto represented.

To my surprise, one of our readers gave that message a completely different slant. She sent a note informing me that her daughter and her daughter's friends—all tennis players—wear shirts with that slogan. In tennis, a "love" score is zero. If your score in a game is "love," you lose—so in tennis, love really is for losers. That mom's note gave me a new perspective on that saying.

This incident reminded me how easy it is to make wrong first judgments. Based on incomplete or inaccurate information, we can jump to wrong conclusions and make poor value judgments about people and situations. And that can cause great hurt to others.

Speaking to people who had misjudged Him, Jesus warned, "Stop judging by mere appearances, but instead judge correctly" (John 7:24). We need to be careful that our judgments are backed up by the right information (the truth) and the right attitude (the compassion of Christ). Try this motto: "Righteous judgment is for winners."

. . .

A snap judgment has a way of becoming unfastened.

Still True Today

Acts 17:16–31

> While Paul was waiting for them in Athens, he was greatly
> distressed to see that the city was full of idols. *Acts 17:16*

The Chester Beatty Library in Dublin, Ireland, has an extensive collection of ancient Bible fragments dating back to the second century AD. One fragment on display is a piece of Acts 17:16.

The message that ancient fragment displays, however, is as contemporary as today's newspaper. It reads, "While Paul was waiting for them in Athens, he was greatly distressed to see that the city was full of idols." Paul was angered by the proliferation of idols in ancient Athens, and I am convinced he would be upset with us today.

Some idols that we see in today's world are different from the ones in Paul's day. Whether it's wealth, fame, power, athletes, entertainers, or politicians, contemporary idols abound. As always, our spiritual enemy, Satan, seeks to lure us away from the Savior to the false worship of idols. Christians are not immune, and thus we must guard our hearts against self-righteous anger toward unbelievers who seem to worship everything but God.

We must also be drawn by Christ's love to reach out to those who don't know Him. Then, like the believers at Thessalonica, they may turn "to God from idols to serve the living and true God" (1 Thessalonians 1:9).

• • •

An idol is anything that takes God's rightful place.

Marked by His Name

Acts 11:19–26

The disciples were called Christians first at Antioch. Acts 11:26

In July 1860, the world's first nursing school opened at St. Thomas Hospital in London. Today that school is part of the King's College, where nursing students are called Nightingales. The school—like modern nursing itself—was established by Florence Nightingale, who revolutionized nursing during the Crimean War. When prospective nurses complete their training, they take the "Nightingale Pledge," a reflection of her ongoing impact on nursing.

Many people, like Florence Nightingale, have had a significant impact on our world. But no one has had a greater effect than Jesus, whose birth, death, and resurrection have been transforming lives for 2,000 years.

Around the world, Christ's name marks those who are His followers, going back to the earliest days of the church. "When [Barnabas] found [Saul], he brought him to Antioch. So for a whole year Barnabas and Saul met with the church and taught great numbers of people. The disciples were called Christians first at Antioch" (Acts 11:26).

We who bear Christ's name identify with Him because we have been changed by His love and grace. We declare to the world that He has made an eternal difference in our lives, and we long for that in the hearts of others too.

• • •

Followers of Christ—Christians—are marked by His name.

What Really Matters

Philippians 2:1–11

In humility value others above yourselves,
not looking to your own interests but each of you
to the interests of the others. Philippians 2:3–4

Two men sat down to review their business trip and its results. One said he thought the trip had been worthwhile because some meaningful new relationships had begun through their business contacts. The other said, "Relationships are fine, but selling is what matters most." Obviously, they had very different agendas.

It is all too easy—whether in business, family, or church—to view others from the perspective of how they can benefit us. We value them for what we can get from them, rather than focusing on how we can serve them in Jesus's name. In his letter to the Philippians, Paul wrote, "Do nothing out of selfish ambition or vain conceit. Rather, in humility value others above yourselves, not looking to your own interests but each of you to the interests of the others" (Philippians 2:3–4).

People are not to be used for our own benefit. Because they are loved by God and we are loved by Him, we love one another. His love is the greatest love of all.

• • •

Joy comes from putting another's needs ahead of our own.

—— Unexpected ——

Matthew 10:35–42

*Whoever finds their life will lose it, and whoever
loses their life for my sake will find it.* Matthew 10:39

In the midday heat of summer, while traveling in the American South, my wife and I stopped for ice cream. On the wall behind the counter we saw a sign reading, "Absolutely No Snowmobiling." The humor worked because it was so unexpected.

Sometimes saying the unexpected has the most effect. Think of this in regard to a statement by Jesus: "Whoever finds their life will lose it, and whoever loses their life for my sake will find it" (Matthew 10:39). In a kingdom where the King is a servant (Mark 10:45), losing your life becomes the only way to find it. This is a startling message to a world focused on self-promotion and self-protection.

In practical terms, how can we "lose our life"? The answer is summed up in the word *sacrifice*. When we sacrifice, we put into practice Jesus's way of living. Instead of grasping for our own wants and needs, we esteem the needs and well-being of others.

Jesus not only taught about sacrifice but He also lived it by giving himself for us. His death on the cross became the ultimate expression of the heart of the King who lived up to His own words: "Greater love has no one than this: to lay down one's life for one's friends" (John 15:13).

• • •

Nothing is really lost by a life of sacrifice. —Henry Liddon

Love for Children

Matthew 18:1–10

"Let the children come to me.
Don't stop them!" *Matthew 19:14 (NLT)*

Thomas Barnado entered the London Hospital medical school in 1865, dreaming of life as a medical missionary in China. Barnado soon discovered a desperate need in his own front yard—the many homeless children living and dying on the streets of London. Barnado determined to do something about this horrendous situation. Developing homes for destitute children in London's east end, Barnado rescued some 60,000 boys and girls from poverty and possible early death. Theologian and pastor John Stott said, "Today we might call him the patron saint of street kids."

Jesus said, "Let the children come to me. Don't stop them! For the Kingdom of Heaven belongs to those who are like these children" (Matthew 19:14 NLT). Imagine the surprise the crowds—and Jesus's own disciples—must have felt at this declaration. In the ancient world, children had little value and were largely relegated to the margins of life. Yet Jesus welcomed, blessed, and valued children.

James, challenged Christ-followers saying, "Pure and genuine religion in the sight of God our Father means caring for orphans . . . in their distress" (James 1:27 NLT). Today, like those first-century orphans, children of every social strata, ethnicity, and family environment are at risk due to neglect, human trafficking, abuse, drugs, and more. How can we honor the Father who loves us by showing His care for these little ones Jesus welcomes?

· · ·

Be an expression of the love of Jesus.

Compassion Fatigue

Matthew 9:35–38

When he saw the crowds, he had compassion on them,
because they were harassed and helpless,
like sheep without a shepherd. *Matthew 9:36*

Anne Frank is well-known for her diary describing her family's years of hiding during World War II. When she was later imprisoned in a Nazi death camp, those with her said that "her tears [for them] never ran dry," making her "a blessed presence for all who knew her." Because of this, scholar Kenneth Bailey concluded that Anne never displayed "compassion fatigue."

Compassion fatigue can be one of the results of living in a badly broken world. The sheer volume of human suffering can numb even the best intentioned among us. Compassion fatigue, however, was not in Jesus's makeup. Matthew 9:35–36 says, "Jesus went through all the towns and villages, teaching in their synagogues, proclaiming the good news of the kingdom and healing every disease and sickness. When he saw the crowds, he had compassion on them, because they were harassed and helpless, like sheep without a shepherd."

Our world suffers not only from physical needs but also from spiritual brokenness. Jesus came to meet that need and challenged His followers to join Him in this work (vv. 37–38). He prayed that the Father would raise up workers to respond to the needs all around us—people who struggle with loneliness, sin, and illness. May the Father give us a heart for others that mirrors His heart. In the strength of His Spirit, we can express His compassionate concern.

• • •

In a world filled with heartache, we can model the compassion of Jesus.

Dangerous Distractions

John 13:31–35

"Your love for one another will prove to the world
that you are my disciples." *John 13:35 (NLT)*

Artist Sigismund Goetze shocked Victorian-era England with a painting entitled "Despised and Rejected of Men." In it, he portrayed the suffering, condemned Jesus surrounded by people of Goetze's own generation. They were so consumed by their own interests—business, romance, politics—that they were shockingly oblivious to the Savior's sacrifice. Indifferent to Christ, the surrounding crowd, like the mob at the foot of Jesus's cross, had no idea what—or who—they had missed.

In our day as well, believers and unbelievers alike can easily become distracted from the eternal. How can followers of Jesus cut through this fog of distraction with the truth of God's great love? We can begin by loving one another as fellow children of God. Jesus said, "Your love for one another will prove to the world that you are my disciples" (John 13:35 NLT).

But real love doesn't stop there. We extend that love by sharing the gospel in hopes of drawing people to the Savior. As Paul wrote, "We are . . . Christ's ambassadors" (2 Corinthians 5:20).

In this way, the body of Christ can both reflect and project God's love, the love we all so desperately need, to each other and to our world. May both efforts, empowered by His Spirit, be a part of cutting through the distractions that hinder us from seeing the wonder of God's love in Jesus.

• • •

To a world living in the fog of distraction,
we bring the light of the good news of Jesus.

The Greatest
Rescue Mission

Luke 19:1–10

The Son of Man came to seek and to save the lost. *Luke 19:10*

On February 18, 1952, a massive storm split the SS *Pendleton*, a tanker ship, into two pieces about ten miles off the Massachusetts coast. More than forty sailors were trapped inside the ship's sinking stern in the midst of fierce winds and violent waves.

When word of the disaster reached the Coast Guard station in Chatham, Massachusetts, Boatswain's Mate First Class Bernie Webber took three men on a lifeboat to try to save the stranded crew against nearly impossible odds—and brought thirty-two of the seemingly doomed sailors to safety. Their courageous feat was deemed one of the greatest rescues in United States Coast Guard history and was the subject of the 2016 film *The Finest Hours*.

In Luke 19:10, Jesus declared His own rescue mission saying, "The Son of Man came to seek and to save the lost." The cross and the resurrection became the ultimate expression of that rescue, as Jesus took upon himself our sins and restored to the Father all who trust Him. For 2,000 years, people have embraced His offer of abundant life now and eternal life with Him. Rescued!

As followers of Jesus we have the privilege, with the Holy Spirit's help, to join our Savior in the greatest rescue mission of all. Who in your life needs His rescuing love?

• • •

Jesus took our sin that we might have His salvation;
He took our place that we might have His peace.

Steel and Velvet

John 8:1–11

"Let any one of you who is without sin
be the first to throw a stone at her." *John 8:7*

Poet Carl Sandburg wrote of former US president Abraham Lincoln, "Not often in the story of mankind does a man arrive on earth who is both steel and velvet, . . . who holds in his heart and mind the paradox of terrible storm and peace unspeakable and perfect." "Steel and velvet" described how Lincoln balanced the power of his office with concern for individuals longing for freedom.

Only one person in all history perfectly balanced strength and softness, power and compassion. That man is Jesus Christ. In John 8, when confronted by the religious leaders to condemn a guilty woman, Jesus displayed both steel and velvet. He showed steel by withstanding the demands of a bloodthirsty mob, instead turning their critical eyes upon themselves. He said to them, "Let any one of you who is without sin be the first to throw a stone at her" (v. 7). Then Jesus modeled the velvet of compassion by telling the woman, "Neither do I condemn you. . . . Go now and leave your life of sin" (v. 11).

Reflecting His "steel and velvet" in our own responses to others can reveal the Father's work of conforming us to be like Jesus. We can show His heart to a world hungry for both the velvet of mercy and the steel of justice.

. . .

Dear Father, I thank you for your Son, whose strength
and tenderness perfectly reveal your heart for our lost world.

Macauley

Isaiah 6:1–8

I heard the voice of the Lord saying, "Whom shall I send?
And who will go for us?" And I said, "Here am I. Send me!" *Isaiah 6:8*

Macauley Rivera, one of my dearest friends in Bible college, had a passion for the Savior. His heart's desire was to graduate, marry his fiancée, Sharon, return to the inner city of Washington, DC, and plant a church to reach his friends and family for Christ.

That dream ended, however, when Mac and Sharon were tragically killed in an accident, leaving the student body stunned at the loss. At Mac's memorial service, the challenge was issued: "Mac is gone. Who will serve in his place?" As evidence of the impact of Mac's example, more than two hundred students stood to take up the mantle of Christ's fallen servant.

The response of those students echoes the commitment of Isaiah. In a time of fear and insecurity, the prophet was summoned into the throne room of God, where he heard Him say, "Whom shall I send? And who will go for us?" Isaiah responded, "Here am I. Send me!" (Isaiah 6:8).

God still calls men and women to be His ambassadors today. He challenges us to serve Him—sometimes close to home, sometimes in distant lands. The question for us is, "How will we respond to His call?" May God give us the courage to say, "Here am I. Send me!"

• • •

Whom God calls, He qualifies; whom He qualifies, He sends.

A Man My Age

Psalm 71

> When I am old and gray, do not forsake me, my God,
> till I declare . . . your mighty acts to all who are to come. *Psalm 71:18*

On a recent flight, I got ready to do some work. Spread out on my tray were my laptop computer, backup hard drive, iPod, and other gadgets that are part of being a twenty-first-century "road warrior." As I worked, a young man seated beside me asked if he could make a comment. He told me how inspirational it was for him, a young man, to see someone my age so enthusiastically embracing modern technology. In spite of his intention to compliment me, I suddenly felt about 120 years old. What did he mean by "someone my age"? I wondered. After all, I was *only* 57.

Then I remembered Psalm 71, the psalm for folks "my age" and beyond. It reminds us of the value of a life well lived and of the worth of lessons learned: Lessons are not just for our benefit but also for us to pass along to the next generations. The psalmist wrote, "When I am old and gray, do not forsake me, my God, till I declare your power to the next generation, your mighty acts to all who are to come" (v. 18).

So, maybe being "someone my age" isn't such a bad gig. It is the privilege of "veteran" Christ-followers to declare the strength and power of God to the younger generations. That's how we can truly be inspirational to them.

• • •

The best gift for the younger generation
is a good example from the older generation.

Doing Good

1 Peter 3:8–17

It is better, if it is God's will,
to suffer for doing good than for doing evil. *1 Peter 3:17*

Joseph (not his real name) was the model of a trusted military officer, rising in his nation's army to the rank of colonel in the special forces. With this came great opportunity, both for good and bad.

When deployed into a region wracked with drug trafficking, Joseph was intent on bringing justice to that plagued area. He and his troops began dealing with the criminals to protect the people. Some of his superiors, who were corrupt and took bribes from the drug runners, ordered him to turn his head to let them move their drugs. He repeatedly refused until he was finally arrested and imprisoned for eight years—for doing good.

Sadly, we live in a world where at times doing good brings suffering. This was true for Joseph; his payment for serving his people was unjust imprisonment.

The apostle Peter, having also been jailed for doing good, understood that kind of heartache. He gave us this perspective: "It is better, if it is God's will, to suffer for doing good than for doing evil" (1 Peter 3:17).

As Joseph shared the stories of what God taught him in prison, I learned that the justice of God is not hampered by the evil of men. Doing good is still pleasing in His sight—even when we're mistreated by the world for it.

• • •

The joy of doing good may be the only reward we receive—
but it's worth it!

The King's Colors

John 13:31–35

"By this everyone will know that you are my disciples,
if you love one another." *John 13:35*

In Thailand, the people greatly loved and admired King Bhumibol (1927–2016), who led them for seventy years. To display their respect for the king, many Thai people wore bright yellow shirts every Monday during his reign, because yellow was the official color of the king.

As we seek to live for our King, the Lord Jesus Christ, we should also show our colors of allegiance and appreciation for all He has done for us. But how? What are the "colors" that declare to the world that we serve the King of kings and Lord of lords?

The night before His crucifixion, King Jesus told us what our "colors" should be when He said, "By this everyone will know that you are my disciples, if you love one another" (John 13:35). His disciple John echoed this when he wrote, "Dear friends, since God so loved us, we also ought to love one another" (1 John 4:11).

When we display Christ's love for our fellow believers, it is more than just kindness or care. It is one of the most tangible ways we can show our love and devotion for the Savior.

As we interact with fellow Christ-followers, let's be sure to show our colors. That will honor our King before a watching world.

• • •

Our love for God shows in our love for others.

Worth Dying For

Philippians 1:19–26

For to me, to live is Christ and to die is gain. *Philippians 1:21*

Sophie Scholl was a young German woman during the 1940s. She saw the deterioration of her country under the iron rule of the Nazi regime, and she determined to make a difference. She and her brother, with a small group of friends, began to peacefully protest not only the actions but also the values that the Nazis had forced upon the nation.

Sophie and others were arrested and executed for speaking out against the evil in their land. Although she wasn't eager to die, she saw that the conditions in her country had to be addressed—even if it meant her death.

Sophie's story raises a critical question for us as well. What would we be willing to die for? In 1956 Jim Elliot, Nate Saint, Pete Fleming, Roger Youderian, and Ed McCully gave their lives in the jungles of South America because they were committed to spreading the gospel. Elliot revealed the heart that drove such sacrifice when he wrote, "He is no fool who gives what he cannot keep to gain that which he cannot lose." The apostle Paul put it this way: "For to me, to live is Christ and to die is gain" (Philippians 1:21).

Some things really are worth dying for—and in them we gain the reward of the One who declares, "Well done, good and faithful servant!" (Matthew 25:21, 23).

• • •

**Those who faithfully bear the cross in this life
will wear the crown in the life to come.**

Worthy of Respect

Philippians 2:19–30

Welcome [Epaphroditus] in the Lord with great joy,
and honor people like him. *Philippians 2:29*

Just before kickoff at Super Bowl XLIII, Kurt Warner of the Arizona Cardinals received the Walter Payton NFL Man of the Year Award—a tribute given to the player who had best combined on-field excellence with off-field community service. "I am humbled the Lord has given me such an amazing life to impact others," said Warner, a dedicated Christian. "Of all the awards given to NFL athletes, [this one] stands out . . . because of what it represents." It represents a commitment to giving and sacrificing for others.

Paying homage to those who serve is not a new concept. Paul spoke of it when he reminded the Philippians to honor people who gave themselves in serving Christ. He told them of their friend Epaphroditus, who had nearly died (Philippians 2:30) because of his efforts for Christ in ministering to others—including the people at Philippi. How should they respond? Paul said, "Welcome him in the Lord with great joy, and honor people like him" (v. 29). Clearly, when we think of those who sacrifice in serving the Savior, they are worthy of our respect and appreciation.

Why not look for ways to show gratitude to those who have served you spiritually. Give them the honor they deserve.

• • •

We honor God when we honor those who serve God.

Why We Work

Ephesians 6:5–9

Obey them not only to win their favor
when their eye is on you, but as slaves of Christ,
doing the will of God from your heart. *Ephesians 6:6*

In the late 1660s, Sir Christopher Wren was commissioned to redesign St. Paul's Cathedral in London. According to legend, one day he visited the construction site of this great edifice and was unrecognized by the workers. Wren walked about the site, asking several of the men what they were doing. One worker replied, "I am cutting a piece of stone." A second worker responded, "I'm earning five shillings two pence a day." A third, however, had a different perspective: "I am helping Christopher Wren build a magnificent cathedral to the glory of God." What a contrast in the attitude and motivation of that worker!

Why we do what we do is extremely important, particularly when it comes to our working lives and careers. That's why Paul challenged the Ephesians to do their work, "not only to win [people's] favor when their eye is on you, but as slaves of Christ, doing the will of God from your heart. Serve wholeheartedly, as if you were serving the Lord, not people" (Ephesians 6:6–7).

If we do our work merely to earn a paycheck or satisfy a supervisor, we will fall short of the highest motivation—doing our best as evidence of our devotion to God. So, why do we work? As that laborer told Wren, we work "to the glory of God."

· · ·

No matter who signs your paycheck,
you are really working for God.

Greek Fire

James 3:1–12

> The tongue also is a fire, a world of evil among the parts of the body. It corrupts the whole body, sets the whole course of one's life on fire, and is itself set on fire by hell. *James 3:6*

Greek fire was a chemical solution that was used in ancient warfare by the Byzantine Empire against its enemies. According to one online source, it was developed around AD 672 and was used with devastating effect, especially in sea warfare because it could burn on water. What was Greek fire? Its actual chemical composition remains a mystery. It was such a valuable military weapon that the formula was kept an absolute secret—and was lost to the ravages of history. Today, researchers continue to try to replicate that ancient formula, but without success.

One source of catastrophic destruction among believers in Christ, however, is not a mystery. James tells us that the source of ruin in our relationships is often a very different kind of fire. He wrote, "The tongue also is a fire, a world of evil among the parts of the body. It corrupts the whole body" (James 3:6). Those strong words remind us how damaging unguarded words can be to those around us.

Instead of creating the kind of verbal "Greek fire" that can destroy relationships, families, and churches, let's yield our tongue to the Holy Spirit's control and allow our words to glorify the Lord.

• • •

To bridle your tongue, give God the reins of your heart.

Never Forsaken

Psalm 22:1–10

Jesus cried out in a loud voice, . . . "My God, my God,
why have you forsaken me?" Matthew 27:46

Russian writer Fyodor Dostoyevsky said, "The degree of civilization in a society can be judged by entering its prisons." With that in mind, I read an online article describing "The Top 8 Deadliest Prisons in the World." In one of these prisons every prisoner is held in solitary confinement.

We are intended to live and relate in relationships and community, not in isolation. This is what makes solitary confinement such a harsh punishment.

Isolation is the agony Christ suffered when His eternal relationship with the Father was broken on the cross. We hear this in His cry captured in Matthew 27:46: "About three in the afternoon Jesus cried out in a loud voice, 'Eli, Eli, lema sabachthani?' (which means, 'My God, my God, why have you forsaken me?')." As He suffered and died under the burden of our sins, Christ was suddenly alone, forsaken, isolated, cut off from His relationship with the Father. Yet His suffering in isolation secured for us the promise of the Father: "Never will I leave you; never will I forsake you" (Hebrews 13:5).

Christ endured the agony and abandonment of the cross for us so we would never be alone or abandoned by our God. Ever.

•   •   •

Those who know Jesus are never alone.

Great Sacrifice

Hebrews 10:5–18

The Lord Jesus Christ . . .
gave himself for our sins to rescue us. *Galatians 1:3–4*

W. T. Stead, an innovative English journalist at the turn of the twentieth century, was known for writing about controversial social issues. Two of the articles he published addressed the danger of ships operating with an insufficient ratio of lifeboats to passengers. Ironically, Stead was aboard the *Titanic* when it struck an iceberg in the North Atlantic on April 15, 1912. According to one report, after helping women and children into lifeboats, Stead sacrificed his own life by giving up his life vest and a place in the lifeboats so others could be rescued.

There is something very stirring about self-sacrifice. No greater example of that can be found than in Christ himself. The writer of Hebrews says, "This Man, after He had offered one sacrifice for sins forever, sat down at the right hand of God. . . . For by one offering He has perfected forever those who are being sanctified" (Hebrews 10:12, 14 NKJV). In his letter to the Galatians, Paul opened with words describing this great sacrifice: "The Lord Jesus Christ . . . gave himself for our sins to rescue us from the present evil age" (1:3–4).

Jesus's offering of himself on our behalf is the measure of His love for us. That willing sacrifice continues to rescue men and women and offer assurance of eternity with Him.

• • •

Jesus laid down His life to show His love for us.

Dwell with Understanding

Ephesians 5:25–33

Husbands . . . be considerate as you live with your wives . . .
so that nothing will hinder your prayers. *1 Peter 3:7*

My wife, Marlene, and I have been married for some forty years, and we have learned to appreciate each other and enjoy each other's unique qualities. But even after all these years she still surprises me from time to time. Recently, she reacted to a news report in a way that was opposite to what I expected. I told her, "Wow, that shocks me. I never would have thought you would land there on this issue." Her response? "Your job is to figure me out, and my job is to keep you guessing!" The responsibility to understand your spouse is what keeps married life interesting and stretching.

This is an ancient challenge. Peter wrote: "Husbands, in the same way be considerate as you live with your wives, and treat them with respect as the weaker partner and as heirs with you of the gracious gift of life, so that nothing will hinder your prayers" (1 Peter 3:7). He saw it as a priority for the husband to become a student of his wife—to know and understand her. Without that commitment to understanding his spouse, a husband is not capable of doing what comes next—honoring her.

As a husband, if I am to love my wife as Christ loves the church (Ephesians 5:25), it will begin with the intentional effort to grow in my understanding of her.

• • •

Marriage thrives in a climate of love and respect.

Of Weeping and Rejoicing

Romans 12:9–16

Rejoice with those who rejoice;
mourn with those who mourn. *Romans 12:15*

Golda Meir knew both struggle and success during her life. As prime minister of Israel, she experienced many episodes of conflict and loss, as well as the periodic joy of successes and victory in the life of the fledgling State of Israel. She said of joy and sorrow, "Those who don't know how to weep with their whole heart, don't know how to laugh either."

The apostle Paul called us to a life of both weeping and rejoicing—but with a twist. In Romans 12:15, the apostle challenged us to look outside our own experiences to the needs of others. He said, "Rejoice with those who rejoice; mourn with those who mourn."

If we rejoice only in our own victories, we miss the wonder of celebrating the power of the Lord, who desires to accomplish His purposes in and through others as well. If we mourn only our own losses, we lose the opportunity to "be there" for those who are hurting by showing them compassion.

Life is filled with the extremes of joy and sorrow, victory and defeat. But we have been given the privilege of entering into those moments in people's lives to see the grace of God at work. Don't miss it!

• • •

Looking to the needs of others honors Christ.

No More; No Less

2 Timothy 2:14–26

*Do your best to present yourself to God as one approved,
a worker who does not need to be ashamed and who
correctly handles the word of truth.* 2 Timothy 2:15

Recently I was reading about how easy it is to mishandle the message of the Bible. We may try to make it support what we already believe is true instead of allowing it to speak to us with God's intended message. Some people use the Bible to defend one side of an issue, while others use the Bible to attack that same issue. Both quote Scripture to support their views, but both can't be right.

It is important as we use God's Word that we are committed to saying no more and no less than the Scriptures actually say. If we mishandle the Word, we misrepresent it, which ultimately misrepresents God's character. This is why Paul challenged Timothy, "Do your best to present yourself to God as one approved, a worker who does not need to be ashamed and who correctly handles the word of truth" (2 Timothy 2:15). A key priority for unashamed, approved workers for Christ is to accurately interpret God's Word. As we study, we can depend on the Spirit, who inspired it, to give us understanding and wisdom.

Through our words and actions, we have opportunity to represent God's Word to others in ways that genuinely reflect God's heart. That is one of the greatest privileges of the Christian life.

• • •

God's Word—handle with care.

The Finish Line

1 Corinthians 9:24–27

Tell Archippus: "See to it that you complete the ministry you have received in the Lord." *Colossians 4:17*

When I was in college, I ran on the cross-country team. In the final event of the season, the state's small colleges competed against each other, with about seventy-five runners in the event. We ran the 5K course in the rain and mud on a cold November day.

As I neared the finish line, I spied a runner from one of the other schools just a short distance ahead of me. He became my goal. I ran as hard as I could and passed him just as I crossed the finish line. That last dash meant I finished forty-second, which seemed a lot better than forty-third! It meant our team finished one position higher in the final standings than the team represented by the runner I beat. The point? I didn't give up—I ran all the way through the finish line.

This is probably what Paul had in mind as he wrote to Archippus, one of his young ministry protégés: "See to it that you complete the ministry you have received in the Lord" (Colossians 4:17). When we feel discouraged and want to quit, it's good to remember that the Lord who entrusted us with the privilege of spiritual service will give us the grace and strength to carry out that service. Let us "run with perseverance" (Hebrews 12:1) so we will receive the "crown that will last forever" (1 Corinthians 9:25).

• • •

Running with patience is perseverance in the "long run."

Also by Bill Crowder

. . .

Help us get the word out!

Our Daily Bread Publishing exists to feed the soul with the Word of God.

If you appreciated this book, please let others know.

- Pick up another copy to give as a gift.
- Share a link to the book or mention it on social media.
- Write a review on your blog, on a book-seller's website, or at our own site (odb.org/store).
- Recommend this book for your church, book club, or small group.

Connect with us:

[Facebook] @ourdailybread

[Instagram] @ourdailybread

[Twitter] @ourdailybread

Our Daily Bread Publishing
PO Box 3566
Grand Rapids, Michigan 49501 USA

[Mail] books@odb.org